A Dirty South Manifesto

AMERICAN STUDIES NOW:
CRITICAL HISTORIES OF THE PRESENT

Edited by Lisa Duggan and Curtis Marez

Much of the most exciting contemporary work in American Studies refuses the distinction between politics and culture, focusing on historical cultures of power and protest on the one hand, or the political meanings and consequences of cultural practices, on the other. *American Studies Now* offers concise, accessible, authoritative books on significant political debates, personalities, and popular cultural phenomena quickly, while such teachable moments are at the forefront of public consciousness.

A Dirty South Manifesto

*Sexual Resistance and Imagination
in the New South*

L. H. Stallings

UNIVERSITY OF CALIFORNIA PRESS

University of California Press
Oakland, California

Library of Congress Cataloging-in-Publication Data
Names: Horton-Stallings, LaMonda, author.
Title: A Dirty South manifesto : sexual resistance and
    imagination in the New South / L.H. Stallings.
Other titles: American studies now ; 10.
Identifiers: LCCN 2019017214 (print) | LCCN 2019022108
    (ebook) | ISBN 9780520299498 (cloth : alk. paper) | ISBN
    9780520299504 (pbk. : alk. paper) | ISBN 9780520971202
    (ebook)
Subjects: LCSH: African American sexual minorities—
    Southern States—21st century. | Sex—Social
    aspects—Southern States—21st century.
Classification: LCC HQ76.27.A37 H67 2020 (print) |
    LCC HQ76.27.A37 (ebook) | DDC 306.70975/0905—dc23
LC record available at https://lccn.loc.gov/2019017214
LC ebook record available at https://lccn.loc.gov/2019022108

Manufactured in the United States of America

28 27 26 25 24 23 22 21 20 19
10 9 8 7 6 5 4 3 2 1

We recognize that in issuing this manifesto we must prepare for a long-range educational campaign in all communities of this country, but we know that the Christian churches have contributed to our oppression in white America.

James Forman, "Black Manifesto"

The manifesto declares a position: the manifesto refuses dialogue or discussion: the manifesto fosters antagonism and scorns conciliation. It is univocal, unilateral, single-minded. It conveys resolute oppositionality and indulges no tolerance for the fainthearted ...

Janet Lyon, *Manifestoes: Provocations of the Modern*

If you are reading this in the United States or Canada, whose land are you on, dear reader? What are the specific names of the Native nation(s) who have historical claim to the territory on which you currently read this article? What are their histories before European invasion? What are their historical and present acts of resistance to colonial occupation? If you are like most people in the United States and Canada, you cannot answer these questions. And this disturbs me.

Qwo-Li Driskill, "Double-Weaving Two-Spirit Critiques"

CONTENTS

OVERVIEW

INTRODUCTION

Defines Dirty South and its relationship to the Old South and New South. Examines the history and purpose of the manifesto as a written genre.

Southern Essentialism · Hip-Hop · Intersectionality · Deviance as Resistance

SLOW TONGUE MANIFESTO / CHAPTER I

Moral authority and calls for a moral revival cannot adequately address sexual and gender equity. Provides techniques for how to read the *Dirty South Manifesto*. Discusses the importance of various forms of literacy to sexual resistance.

Millie Jackson · Slow Tongue · Moral Mondays · Reverend William Barber

DIRT MANIFESTO / CHAPTER 2

The metaphorical and cultural significance of obscenity for lesbian writers and activists and contemporary publishers. Discusses the importance of lesbian imagination and obscenity among teachers and activists on college campuses, as well as intergenerational coalitions, to sexual resistance.

Lesbian Imagination · Sinister Wisdom · Audre Lorde · Ann Allen Shockley · Cocks Not Glocks

GEOPHUKIT MANIFESTO / CHAPTER 3

Settler colonialism shapes southern politics around gender and sexuality. Land politics and grassroots organizing in regards to issues related to interracial sex, sexual commerce, and decriminalization of sex work demonstrate this.

Geophagia · Adam and Eve · The Occaneechi · Women with a Vision

T.R.A.P (THE RATCHET ALLIANCE FOR PROSPERITY) MANIFESTO / CHAPTER 4

Targeted regulation of abortion providers has decreased access to abortion throughout some southern states. Other issues in reproductive justice, such as LGBT adoptions, the HIV/AIDS epidemic, and access to birth control, remain at stake due to defunding of Planned Parenthood. Southern community organizations' bold approaches.

TRAP · Reproductive Justice · Midwifery · Women's Health Movement · SisterSong

WEUSIOURU FUTURE PRONOUNS MANIFESTO / CHAPTER 5

Southern legislatures' attempt to solidify biological sex assigned at birth as the only recognizable form of gender in order to counter gender fluidity. These bills demonstrate the links between class, gender, and exploitative labor practices. Music by three figures counters these ideologies.

Gospel Singer Little Axe · Rapper Big Momma · Bounce Music Innovator Big Freedia

HONEYSUCKLE, NOT HONEY SUCKA!
MANIFESTO / CODA

There must be a larger investment in the arts, which remain important to the futurity of sexuality, because they develop imaginative practices that become the basis of the underground movements necessary in a sexual dystopia.

Gloria Anzaldúa · Gayl Jones · From Vice to ICE Campaign

Introduction

The New South is the epicenter of neoteric sex wars, technologies, and economies. Issues of reproductive freedom, criminalization of sexual practices, HIV/AIDS, partner rights and marriage equality, and transgender rights reveal how southern states have entered into another era of reconstruction centered on sexuality and gender. This New South strategizes sexual violence and terrorism into policies about education, immigration, wage labor, and economic development: not unlike the Old South's previous era of crafting Black Codes and Jim Crow, it continues to depend upon anti-Blackness, sexual morality, and dehumanization of the poor for its growth and support. Yet, there is a great deal of resistance in the New South made evident by the strategies and missions of movements including SONG (Southerners on New Ground), SisterSong, Women with a Vision, BreakOUT!, Black Lives Matter chapters, Moral Mondays, and sanctuary movements. Thus, this book understands and reiterates that sexual resistance is already happening. It celebrates, examines, and highlights the various modes that resistance has taken and the possible future directions it may take.

While persons living in southern states typically classified under the broad rubric of "the South" know that there is not one South but many, there are historical narratives that have ignored the development of multiple Souths. Recent developments in southern studies unravel essentialist ideas of "the South." Some of the essentialisms being challenged include agrarianism, Christian-centricity, singular public/political identity linked with the Confederacy, racial binary of Black/white, and genteel men and women. In explaining their concerted scholarly effort to bring southern studies and global studies into conversation with each other, Deborah Cohn and Jon Smith state that "constructions of southern identity offered by white male southerners, from the Confederate flag to ... the canon of southern literature, themselves constitute exclusionary and exceptionalist myths ... [and] figure (white) southern culture and history as a corrective to provincial hubris of the imperial United States."[1] Likewise, historian Jane Landers insists that southern studies scholars "do a better job of incorporating the lives of the many non-Europeans who formed the majority population as they reshape the history of the Southeast."[2] These scholars attend to the issues of nationalism and whiteness dominating understandings of southern identity. Sociologist Zandria Robinson knows that there are also risks in using Black authenticity to outline the parameters of the Dirty South, explaining, "From the plays, films, and television shows of writer and producer Tyler Perry ... to hip-hop's music definitive turn toward crunk and the Dirty South, the South has risen again as the geographic epicenter of authentic Black identity."[3] Outside of academia, various cultural creators of the Dirty South have done exactly that, while also grappling with other forms of essentialism. Explicitly, the whiteness of southern identity and exceptionalism is confronted within the Dirty South. Implicitly, even when they are espoused, authentic and essentialist ideals of blackness are not sustained in Dirty South cultural production as a result of intersections of gender, sexuality, and geographical regionalisms.

As this book is entitled *A Dirty South Manifesto,* readers of a particular generation will see the influence of southern hip-hop culture. Because Dirty South music helped many survive the oppressive state policies around class, race, gender, and sexuality signed into existence during the two terms of former president William Jefferson Clinton (1993–2001) from Arkansas, this manifesto is without a doubt inspired by southern hip-hop genres of booty bass, crunk, trap, and bounce music created or cultivated by artists such as 2 Live Crew, Geto Boys, Master P, UGK, OutKast, Ludacris, Justus League, Little Brother, Juvenile, Lil Wayne, TI, Lil Jon, Trick Daddy, and Trina. In Georgia, Dr. Regina Bradley and Dr. Bettina Love have been going about the work of institution building for southern hip-hop. Bradley, the author of a collection of short stories entitled *Boondock Kollage: Stories from the Hip Hop South* and the forthcoming book *Chronicling Stankonia: OutKast and the Rise of the Hip Hop South,* remains convinced that southern hip-hop contains lessons as valuable as those of trickster tales, folklore, and mother wit for a post-Civil Rights generation. Love's *Hip Hop's Li'l Sistas Speak: Negotiating Hip Hop Identities and Politics in the New South* examines the significance of hip-hop to Black girlhood identity and insists upon its usefulness as a pedagogical tool in urban classroom spaces. Not so quietly, they have been going off about the value of southern hip-hop and righteously so. Years earlier, the Crunk Feminist Collective, cofounded by Brittney Cooper and Susana

Morris, linked hip-hop, regionalism, and concerns of gender and sexuality. These stalwarts pay attention to the political impetus, as well as the urgency of aesthetics, in the Dirty South's refusals of an essentialist Black identity rooted in Black heteronormative masculinity. Thus, this book joins previous work in comprehending the significance of southern hip-hop to political and artistic imagination, as well as to the terrain of sexuality and gender studies. It intends to destabilize southern essentialisms based in white patriarchy and racialized class myths.

As outlined in the following chapters, I am specifically guided by the fecundity of "dirt" (dirty imagination), a different, older set of sonic aesthetic practices sampled in southern hip-hop music, and by one persistent metaphor and analytic framework—the intersection—as well as by how the practice of intersectional politics is often offered as a solution for challenging the anti-Black, pro-patriarchal state to make institutional practices about gender and sexuality more equitable. This short book attends to an irresolvable factor within aboveground political movements whose foundation is intersectionality: the delimitation placed on the concept of intersectionality and the practice of intersectional politics by an unacknowledged prior foundational commitment to moral authority that is neither gender neutral, sexually apolitical, antiracist, atheistic, nor agnostic.

Therefore, the book metaphorically highlights the imaginative off-road routes, shortcuts, side streets, dirt roads, and secret paths that might be located at, near, or surrounding the intersection, to think through its shortcomings when we think about what exists in the interim of policy and legislation. I highlight how the Dirty South's aesthetics and artistic critique of moral authority disengage from the boundaries of legal discourse and public policy established by regional differences and markers of gender and sexuality. The book embraces the still-useful phrase, "the dirty," since in its finest and filthiest iterations it exists as the simultaneous place and practice of intersectional politics, critiques of moral authority, and the development of regional aesthetic philosophies whose purpose is dismantling and reinventing southern public spheres largely erected out of the sexual economy of slavery and sustained by settler colonialism.

With this inspiration in mind, I provide several minor Dirty South manifestos to address individual issues that comprise the larger completed manifesto. I then offer explanations for why particular tactics in the manifesto might be necessary based on case studies taken from contemporary southern life. By focusing on Black communities and their construction of the Dirty South, I rejoice in the roots of radical sexual politics and cultural imagination in the New South before discussing their significance to the U.S. political landscape. I do so by placing Black communities' politics and efforts in conversation with those of other racially and sexually marginalized communities. Through an exploration of how some Black communities recognize the previously mentioned racialized elements of southern gender and sexual politics, and their countering of such politics with radical investment in arts and culture, I underscore the invention of cultural economies that shift the ideological ground upon which sexual moral panics in the South emerge. Unfortunately, it does not comprehensively attend to all issues regarding gender and sexual resistance in the South. Pressing concerns such as sexuality and disability, child and adolescent sexual education, and HIV/AIDS are not explicitly covered as stand-alone chapters, but the arguments of the chapters and manifestos are applicable to those issues and communities.

Because contemporary southern politics and public spheres have produced sexual moral panics, I offer a manifesto culled from dirty moments of political or cultural resistance, which combat the sexual conservatism that continues to harm racial, gendered, and sexual minorities. As Janet Lyon has written, "to write a manifesto is to announce one's participation, however discursive, in a history of struggle against oppressive forces."[4] Historically, manifestos have been used in a variety of ways: as inspiration for radicalizing politics, a way to share cultural insights and innovations, or as means to build and locate a communal space for new social being. They can be political, scientific, aesthetic, or technical. The manifesto's function as a guerilla form of writing and slow studying is even more important in the era of inhuman pace established by digital speed and space that is the worldwide web. Manifestos direct us to numerous and various figures, books, and texts to study for self or with others. Despite the function of the manifesto in the modern public sphere, Lyon does note several conflicting issues within the form: universalism, the signature pronoun "we," the difficulty of a collective self-representation, gendered imperatives derived from masculinist revolutionary discourse, and rigid hierarchical binaries.[5] Southern manifestos have typically been centered on racial segregation and white nationalism, as opposed to sexuality and gender.[6] However, *A Dirty South Manifesto* insists that sexual liberation and gender fluidity can also shape ongoing efforts to achieve racial and class equality, while also critiquing geographical sexual identity politics, antifeminism, and trans-respectability politics. *A Dirty South Manifesto* is modeled after themes and stylistic elements utilized in southern hip-hop, *Black Manifesto* (1969) by James Forman, and *Black Woman's Manifesto* (1970) by the Third World Alliance, as well as elements from the *S.C.U.M. Manifesto* and the *Dada Manifesto*. In addition, it echoes the theoretical and political impetus of the *Communist Manifesto*,

The Empire Strikes Back: A Posttransexual Manifesto, and *A Cyborg Manifesto.*

My contribution to the American Studies Now series intends to offer a discussion about revising the ideals of a public sphere and public good that underwrite the democratic foundations shaping public policy. Using the thesis of political scientist Cathy Cohen, I "take seriously the possibility that in the space created by deviant discourse and practice, especially in Black communities, a new radical politics of deviance could emerge. It might take the shape of a radical politics of the personal, embedded in more recognized Black counter publics, where the most marginal individuals in Black communities, with an eye on the state and other regulatory systems, act with the limited agency available to them to secure small levels of autonomy in their lives."[7] I embrace Cohen's call for a public politics of deviance as a counter to what is being called for in the New South (moral revival and moral authority), as well as outline its necessity to something less public, a belowground movement. I also align myself with Deborah Vargas, who "situate[s] the queer analytic of *lo sucio* in relation to contemporary neoliberal projects that disappear the most vulnerable and disenfranchised by cleaning up spaces and populations deemed dirty and wasteful."[8] Vargas reminds us to think about such questions from the perspective of the land before it is monetized. Thus, I discuss the impact that breaking with settler colonialism and settler sexuality may have on racial and sexual minorities in the New South.

Doing this work from the perspective of the land is a recursive strategy meant to keep in mind one question that is critical to sexual resistance in the New South: Is intersectionality dirty enough for the social justice needs of cisgender, transgender, and queer folk in the South? Intersectionality has been crucial in contemporary social justice movements and considerations of race, gender, class, and nation. Nevertheless, local geographies and the distinct narratives of moral authority they produce reveal the limitations of a policy-based intersectional approach. Honing in on cultural origins of the practice long before Crenshaw's articulation of it in legal discourse may help. Intersectionality remains a political strategy reliant upon moral authority, but community strategies more skeptical of the state are often imagined from alternative perspectives so as to address the moral narrative going unchallenged in the aboveground movements of southern sexual liberation.

At times, this book eschews going public for going underground, forming secret societies and networks, and using models of Black intellectual and imaginative cultures to do so when political and cultural rhetoric of our current era insists upon the good of public intellectuals, institutions, and modes of protest. In spite of capitalism's dehumanization of living beings and its merciless privatization of every natural resource and community institution, such rhetoric relies upon ideals of a universal humanity and outdated notions of a public good and public space. *A Dirty South Manifesto* does not assume that there are not already multiple underground movements. Rather, it honors the different approaches they may take. Arguably, in writing and publishing these words, there is no way to avoid the perils of publicness. But I won't make it easy for all y'all or 'nem who yearn for publicness on behalf of the state's surveillance and appropriation purposes. You will need a decoder ring, a password, a codex, a unique kind of map, and a new type of math to fully decipher the meaning left behind in the book. Its manifestos demand performance and translation to multiple readers and audiences. You will need to closely read what comes before and after the manifestos to fully comprehend the message. You will need to meditate on what is clear and accessible as much as you will need to mark and remark upon what requires clarification. You will need to argue their uselessness/usefulness with self, parents and grandparents, nieces and nephews, lovers and friends, and comrades and community. On the other hand, them so like the CIA cointeling their way through the long twentieth century, be warned that it will require a psychic core of COINTEL spies, linguists fluid in Ebonics, and witches to brew, hoodoo, and conjure for the enemy to understand and fracture what this text is calling for, what this text is moving toward, and what subject this text is seeking out.

By definition manifestos are public declarations announcing political or aesthetic movements, but what they inspire or call forth can be interior, private, and covert forms of insurgency and resistance. As a genre, the manifesto is a text suited for dystopias. Currently, a new wave of hatred threatens to return the South to a Reconstruction fantasy of white supremacy revivalism for misogynist and bigoted men and women, as well as a dystopia for women of color, poor white women, and queer and transfolk. Such a sexual dystopia requires many marginalized people to figure out how to live and reform it from within and from below. Though dystopias are said to be imagined places where people live dehumanized lives and the fantasy of democracy known as America insists that our current reality is not a dystopia, planning strategies of resistance from this imagined place has become most useful in the realities of southern geographies and of the beings living in the margins of those geographies. The manifestos are written based on the South as a sexual dystopia, since this positionality is what the innovators of the Dirty South have used as the basis of their world-making and cultural creations. For those marginalized by colonial regimes of sex and gender and the racially oppressed within these economically disenfranchised segments of society, the South has been a sexual dystopia. For individuals who have ever imagined their freedom as different from an afterlife contingent upon the whims of moral turpitude within white supremacist patriarchy's greed, I hope you find your praise song or your calling in any part of *A Dirty South Manifesto*.

Slow Tongue Manifesto

A distinctive manifestation of colonization is gendered and sexual dis-ease of the tongue. The compulsion to speak and write about sexual resistance and freedom is a manifestation of sexual and gendered decolonization. Manifestations are recursive. The gerund *manifesting* is a willful refusal of linear time and mapped space. Because I believe the words that I write have been manifested elsewhere... Because I believe the words that I speak and write manifest what I imagine, no matter how absurd, I risk failure, misunderstanding, skepticism, dismissal, and disbelief from any reader.

Come. Let us enact freedom and marronage through sexual manifesting. Certain about what is being done. Uncertain that it has not been done before. Unsure if there is even a beginning, middle, or end to this manifestation, manifesting, and manifesto.

.

CHAPTER ONE

Congress shall make no law respecting an
establishment of religion, or prohibiting the free
exercise thereof; or abridging the freedom of
speech ... and to petition the Government for a
redress of grievances.

Amendment I, Constitution of the United States

(a) *Findings* The Congress find that—
(2) laws "neutral" toward religion may burden
religious exercise as surely as laws intended to
interfere with religious exercise

Religious Freedom Restoration Act, 42
U.S. Code §21 B

The white Christian churches are another form of
government in this country and they are used by the
government of this country to exploit the people of
Latin America, Asia, and Africa, but the day is soon
coming to an end.

James Forman, *Black Manifesto*

In the era of Donald Trump's presidency, it seems clear that the
First Amendment ain't, nor ever was, for everybody. The current threat to free speech, alongside the language of religious
freedom, signals why discussion of sexual resistance and imagination should begin with an examination of language and its

impact on how sexual resistance is articulated, organized, and communicated. Gender and sexual resistance in the New South requires a critical skepticism of the U.S. Constitution and any subsequent local and state legislation enacted in defense and preservation of settler religion. Development and passing of bills based on the Religious Freedom Restoration Act, which was signed into existence by former President Clinton in 1993, demonstrate the importance of Forman's warning. Forman, the former SNCC organizer, argues that religious institutions have become another form of government. Though the original federal bill was introduced because the federal government was accused of ignoring non-Christians' religious freedom, it has now become a model for twenty-one states to develop state religious freedom restoration acts that reinscribe localized monotheistic religions' hierarchies of gender and sexual ideology. Religious freedom, then, becomes a tactic by which to discriminate against gender and sexual minorities through house bills or redirection of public funding away from policies that could save the lives of gender and sexual minorities. Though not all states passing these bills are southern, the majority of states enacting such legislation are southern. These state religious freedom restoration acts have become the basis of the HB-blues and HB-bounce, or House Bill blues and bounce for women, children, and sexual minorities. Throughout this chapter, I discuss how current calls by southern leaders for a moral revival alongside increased attempts to develop and pass religious freedom acts suggest the necessity of alternative tactics and strategies based on literacy practices not developed from the country's founding documents or importation of foreign religion.

In journalist Justin Miller's illuminating conversation with Reverend William Barber, the person he notes as the "architect of the Moral Mondays," readers learn about the charismatic, gifted speaker and natural leader.[1] Barber, who was once president of the NAACP North Carolina chapter, took the Democratic National Convention by storm in 2016 with his remarks on faith and morality as the guiding force needed for the country. Barber has sharpened his focus on the current tide of moral conservatives in the South, explaining, "Right now in this country, the real battle is over the South, because the extremists who want to take us backwards, they still play their dog-whistle politics in the South."[2] This manifesto is in complete agreement with Barber: the South is where important battles are being waged.

From obscenity laws and marriage acts to gender apartheid, sexual commerce, and reproductive rights, regulation of sexuality in the United States has been predominantly shaped by and largely dependent upon safeguarding or interpreting the First Amendment, which protects freedom of speech and expression of religion. In turn, histories of sexuality movements and strategies of sexual resistance demonstrate a similar reliance on these rights in political rhetoric and policy reform: from modes of public protest (boycotts, riots, marches, petitions, sit-ins, street blockages) to voting participation around bills informed by gender/sexual identity politics to acceptance of rights rhetoric and a moral authority that sustains a manifest destiny nation and its founding documents. Sexual resistance that is not anti-Black involves a process of sexual decolonization that cannot adhere to this model, even if its publicness evolves from such a framework. As Frantz Fanon exposed, the strengths of nationalism and spontaneity will never be enough: "You'll never overthrow the terrible enemy machine, and you won't change human beings if you forget to raise the standard of consciousness of the rank-and-file. Neither stubborn courage nor fine slogans are enough."[3] Reactionary response from the wretched in matters of sexuality is not a sustainable approach to revolt and rebellion against colonial regimes of gender and sexuality. Sexual decolonization remains important to developing new modes of resistance. The challenge for progenitors of sexual resistance and sexual decolonization is how to advocate for thinking and feeling before acting in a twenty-first century that demands immediate response, lack of feeling, and automation. Learning and unlearning the enslaved and colonial logics of sexuality are not instantaneous or a singular event. Learning and unlearning are slow processes.

Language and rhetoric are as important to sexual resistance in the era of Black Lives Matter as they have been to racial and ethnic resistance in movements related to abolition of slavery, to Reconstruction, and to Civil Rights. The recovery or relearning of African and Indigenous languages cannot erase the harmful ways in which forced language practices shaped how Indigenous and enslaved populations assimilated into gender and sexual practices they did not author or narrate in their own tongue. How does one resist or revolutionize when the very element that needs to be resisted, spiritual conversion that incorporates moral authority, is typically understood as a form of salvation for church or state? As an answer, I highlight how practices and expressions within Black culture contain literacies about gender and sexuality that differ from those within English-language national rights discourses and disavow moral authoritarianism.

In this chapter, I juxtapose Black southern R & B literacy practices and rhetorical tropes used to usurp moral authority in the 1970s against current calls for a moral revival in the contemporary Moral Mondays movement, since the first is an oppositional response to Civil Rights strategies of respectability politics and the latter is influenced by Civil Rights strategies.

HOW TO READ THE MANIFESTOS AND RESIST THE PERILS OF MORAL AUTHORITY

Since these manifestos are about aesthetics as much as politics, the first manifesto—the Slow Tongue Manifesto—attends to form and aesthetics. Manifesto authors typically advocate for some type of literacy in order to fully grasp, comprehend, utilize, and then teach a manifesto. So, let me state it plainly: we need to know how to read these manifestos to understand these manifestos. Because sexual education in the United States is neither comprehensive nor liberatory, a primary process in sexual resistance has entailed heralding literacy practices that are written, oral, visual, and performative. As simple as it sounds, (il)literacy forms the basis of beliefs, miseducation, or knowledge about gender and sexuality. As enslaved Africans and their descendants in the Americas learned languages different than their mother tongues, their shared communal literacy practices weren't simply focused on learning English, Spanish, or Portuguese letters and systems of grammar. These communities also ascertained how to share, translate, and adapt multiple forms and mediums of their own languages and cultures into foreign languages and vice versa so as to survive displacement and ensure freedom. From forged passes and escape paths etched in outhouses and quilts to reading newspapers of abolitionist activism and other possible slave rebellions, multiliteracy was understood as central to physical escape not simply as formal education geared toward upward class mobility. The secretive and criminalized practice of acquiring literacy ensured it as a coveted skill, but it also ensured a range of subversive tactics for how to approach freedom. Sexual literacy as a practice of resistance and freedom is at the heart of this Dirty South manifesto. Sexual resistance movements have emphasized and must continue to emphasize how the creation of different texts and the acquiring of multimodal literacy skills (embodied, affective, discursive, oral, sensorial, and cognitive) produce skills of survival and worldmaking. Knowing how to read, write, and feel a range of texts on and about what has been constructed as gender and sexuality in various communities, and in multiple languages, can assist gender and sexual revolutionaries from being distracted by an underlying singular narrative of moral authority where illiteracy structures oppressive policies.

To understand the role of literacy in sexual resistance in the [text obscured] lo four things: listen to and refuse to be [text obscured] ongue, practice the slow tongue, devise [text obscured] down, and become connoisseurs of dirt. [text obscured] apped by sound and sexual cultures, a [text obscured] tongue will not only save your life; it will make the life saved worth living. A South mapped by sound and sexual culture makes the most sense given the economic changes from agrarian to industrial and energy economies, and from industrial to pharmaceutical, digital, and medical. Birth certificates and citizenship narratives, then, are replaced with life certificates, with line entries that utilize information from new maps charted via histories of labor, as well as with vinyl records that provide a record of origins and existence for people and their modes of resistance—arrangements of notes and archives of sound, material entries from which to break open someone else's lyrics, song, or narrative structure about what it means to be a good or natural citizen or righteous human being.

Snort in disbelief if you dare, but in 2017 the number one producer of pork foods and hog farms, Smithfield Foods, founded in Virginia in 1932, was also one of the top producers of the lifesaving drug heparin. Extracted from pig intestines, heparin is an effective anticoagulant. Smithfield Foods, under the rhetoric of sustainability and "food responsibility," recently expanded into Smithfield Bioscience. Together, they intend to make use of swine in ways previously unimagined: from immunology to tissue regeneration and organ transplants.[4] Ironically, this is the same company that—unsurprisingly, given that many states in the southern United States are right-to-work states—fought against workers' unionization for almost two decades in its North Carolina plants.[5] With its new futuristic and profitable mission, Smithfield Bioscience will not only be writing a new chapter of economic industry in the South, but will also be rewriting what it means to be human and animal, probably without ever shifting the regional narrative of morality and moral authority being challenged in this book. This is the New South, but it is also the Dirty South. Akin to Smithfield's model of sustainability science, this manifesto illuminates sonic sustainability to counter dominant southern politics with their fixed moral stance against gender and sexuality fluidity. Some southerners have been producing a soundtrack to accompany what is coming, and others know that the marginalized and dispossessed require literacy practices situated in techniques of the arts to produce an imagination that will facilitate their survival and liberation. Radical sexual resistance in the twenty-first century South begins with a slow tongue, and there is no better theorization of a slow tongue than that provided by Georgia native Mildred Virginia Jackson otherwise known as Millie Jackson, someone southern hip-hop has sampled over the years.

SLOW: WHEN A MOTHER TONGUE BECOMES
A SLOW TONGUE

Millie Jackson is a living, breathing Dirty South Manifesto. Her entire oeuvre establishes evidence for Cohen's thesis about what a politics of deviance can make possible, as when Cohen notes that "through these attempts to find autonomy, these individuals, with relatively little access to dominant power, not only counter or challenge the presiding normative order with regard to family, sex, and desire, but also create new or counter normative frameworks by which to judge behavior."[6] As Luther Campbell, a.k.a. Uncle Luke, noted some time ago of Jackson's influence on 2 Live Crew's sound and style: "Millie was the first person I ever heard sing like that.... So I said let's do some comedy shit like that."[7] The Miami bass sound and comedic brand of rap was the earliest commercially successful southern rap, as well as the earliest prosecuted for obscenity charges. As Campbell noted, in addition to her rap skills, Jackson's innovations came through in her comedic approaches to themes around sexuality and love: an approach that would show up in other southern hip-hop artists' music. Jackson gave R & B listeners a dynamic conceptual album about sexuality and morals from the perspective of a woman: *Caught Up* (1974). The eight-song album, recorded in Muscle Shoals Studios in Alabama and Criteria Studios in Miami, was a perfect contrast to the new respectability politics bought on by the Civil Rights movement and based in the organizing strategies of the Southern Christian Leadership Conference, which eventually resulted in legal, if not actual, racial integration of American publics. Some critics might argue it was instead *I Had to Say It* (1980), her rap parody of the Sugar Hill Gang, but it was Jackson's musical opus about an adulterous affair told from the point of view of the mistress on one side and the wife on the other, that cemented Jackson as an R & B force and foremother of women's rap in hip-hop culture and southern hip-hop and earned her a Grammy nomination. I open with the genealogical tracing of the Dirty South by way of Millie Jackson specifically because it is her sound of the South, her sonic innovation and narrative bravado that will shape all of my Dirty South manifestos.

Jackson's sound inventions derive from sonic elements expressed on *Caught Up* and her later works, *Feeling Bitchy* (1977) and *E.S.P. (Extra Sexual Persuasion)* (1983). Jackson exposed the production that went into manufacturing an "appropriate" gendered sound for her first album, *Millie Jackson* (1972), telling interviewer Carl Wiser, "In fact, my first album is not my natural voice. They speeded up my voice, it was too low for a woman they thought, so they speeded up all my tracks a half a step, so everything would be higher than I actually sing it in."[8] Nevertheless, what Jackson does with natural vocals on her later albums is a precursor to a technique known in hip-hop as a chopped or screwed sound. Pioneered by Robert Earl Davis, a.k.a. DJ Screw, chopped and screwed music entails deejays slowing down the tempo to skip beats, hesitate or pause, or scratch, as well as taking the pitch of a singer's voice down and stretching it out to create texture. As DJ Screw once stated, "The Screw sound is when I mix tapes with songs that people can relax to . . . . Slower tempos, to feel the music and so you can hear what the rapper is saying. I make my tapes so that everyone can feel them."[9] For contemporary producers this automated technique may have been about synthesizing a mode of chilling or a drug effect, but for Jackson and others, analog or natural slowed-down tempo and lowered and husky vocal dismantle gender binaries. They also invite intimacy in the forms of verbal seduction and dancing—the drag, sexual foreplay, or sexual intercourse. In her performances, Jackson not only provided instruction for sexual acts and relationships, she taught her listeners how to approach the dangers, fears, pleasures, and controversies that arise from the subject of sexuality. She provided rhetorical strategies for debates and arguments around the practice of sexual resistance and sexual freedom—the slow tongue. Part of the problem with how sexuality is taken up in public discourses and institutions arises because the rhetorical strategies being deployed in sexual politics are inadequate in translating the multidimensional and shifting cultural foundations that construct gender or sexuality.

While Sojourner Truth, Frederick Douglass, and Frances Harper may have developed oratory practices essential to the abolition of slavery, and Ida B. Wells, Martin Luther King, and Malcolm X might have devised rhetorical practices crucial to Reconstruction and Civil Rights, their subject was not sexual freedom and sexual resistance. Sexual resistance requires and demands oratory, written, and visual practices powerful enough to shift the imagination of its potential rebels beyond current realities shaped by either a necessity of secrecy, a preference for discretion, a psychological paralysis of stigma, or the criminalization of practices or bodies. The varied possibilities of sexual resistance require the slow tongue.

The first lesson offered by Jackson's instruction on the slow tongue concerns broadening perspective, which entails shifting viewpoints on a singular issue, back and forth, in a performed conversation, so as to illuminate and overcome multiple and contradictory standpoints arising from a moral conflict manufactured by society rather than one's self. The second lesson is to prioritize women's perspectives from multiple locations. The third lesson is to take pleasure in what is being said and how it is being said.

Take for example when Jackson covered country superstar Merle Haggard's 1977 chart-topper "If We're Not Back in Love by Monday." Originally a honky-tonk country song with an up-tempo beat, Jackson's version, released in the same year, makes a marked shift in tempo and title. In Jackson's cover, "If You're Not Back in Love by Monday," the pronoun is changed from *we* to *you*. The pronoun usage shifts the song from a shared labor of loving, putting the onus on one person, who may have messed up and must now take responsibility for repairing the relationship. In this sense, the track becomes an ultimatum, or as I argue, a declaration against the assigned emotional labor and debt of sexual morality charged to women. Her voice and band became the embodied technology and corporeal instruments used to screw Haggard's song from Bakersville country to bluesy R & B. Husky voice, southern drawl, and different breathing cadences are the way she changed the song. Jackson organically exemplifies the effect of a slow tongue. What her cadence allows to surface between each beat, breath, and word are fleeting moments of emotion, ranging from hurt and pain to vulnerability and strength.

Alternatively, the taboo subject matter of good cunnilingus prompted Jackson's delivery of lengthy, humorous songs like "All the Way Lover," in which she sings over a Muscle Shoals beat for ten minutes. It also motivated her six minutes of erotic sound confabulation in "Slow Tongue," which arguably sets the stage for the hip-hop generation's appreciation of blue humor and the elevation of DJ Screw's chopped and screwed sound. "Slow Tongue," on the *E.S.P.* album, is when Jackson perfected embodied organic screwed sound, with pitched-down, molasses lyrical flow. Every sound she produced in singing and moaning was meant to texturally expand the explicit descriptions of sex within lyrics such as, "Frantic, racing heartbeats. Not a love fold left unexplored. Juicy ... lubricating." The huskiness of Jackson's voice provided a serious articulation of nonprocreative sexual pleasure and sonic space for gender androgyny that Donna Summer's 1975 high-pitched fantastic disco tune of melodic moaning, "Love to Love You Baby," might make difficult.

Some critics seemed less impressed with "Slow Tongue." One *Village Voice* critic stated that "the preposterous 'Slow Tongue' is obviously just the faked orgasm that follows the faked foreplay of the title cut."[10] Yet, as Luther Campbell's earlier statement made clear, Jackson's comedic approach to material was something very much valued in Black southern cultures. She most significantly conceptualizes humor as foreplay, aphrodisiac, and erotic exploration. Thus, for Jackson, even when there is humor and parody, there is no such thing as fake orgasm or fake foreplay: humor and parody are themselves forms of sexual pleasure, play, and instruction. Minutes before the song's arrangement of the outro orgasm, Jackson had lyrically coaxed her lover's tongue down her body and coaxed the listener's ear into an orgy of aural erotics. The vocal climax toward the end of the song, alternating between silky singing and rough shouting, is far from a fake anything. Jackson's slow tongue delivers an eargasm. Jackson's performative expressions cannot be mired by self-consciousness and inhibition about the body if she is to elicit a particular response from the audience—devoted following. "Slow Tongue" is the beginning of a significant component of chopped and screwed sound, as well as a configuration of alternative literacy practices for gender and sexuality gifted to emerging generations.

Jackson's later work has seldom been discussed for its genre blurring and aesthetic experimentation. Her experimentation matters to current configurations of Dirty South culture and politics around queer collaborations in contemporary popular Black music: Big Freedia and Lil Wayne, Big Freedia and Beyonce, or Big Freedia and Drake. In Jackson's live album / stage show, *Young Man, Older Woman,* she replaces her traditional breaks, in which she raps to listeners about her desire or love for a younger man, with interludes and skits featuring a drag queen narrator, Chocolate Thunder Montague. In addition to this narration, Jackson includes performed therapy sessions to set up the psychological reason for each song.[11] In form, style, and sound, Millie Jackson demanded that the New South learn to practice the slow tongue to resist the conservative narrative of sexual immorality and moral authority operating in southern culture and Black respectability politics. Such lessons matter most when there are calls for a moral revival in the twenty-first century South.

DOES MORAL AUTHORITY READ, AND IF SO, WHAT TEXTS?

Resisting the perils of moral authority means letting go of some the ways in which racial and sexual resistance has been articulated and strategized in the past. It means unlearning colonial practices and practicing decolonial approaches to sexual revolt and resistance. It requires us to locate foundational texts that are not the U.S. Constitution or the Judeo-Christian Bible. The spiritual conversion of Indigenous, Black, and brown people continues day to day in the realm of the sexual. The acceptance of religious doctrines that separate body and mind from spirit while also creating secular and sacred oppositions in culture and politics has been most effective in oppressing groups of people.

Even before the Memphis-born preacher Reverend Jasper Williams delivered his controversial comments about gender and sexuality in his eulogy for the deceased soul singer Aretha Franklin, voices from the Black pulpit had already demonstrated a lack of care and empathy for the lives of women and sexual minorities placed in jeopardy because of state policies involving health and welfare, as well as hate-based violence stemming from misogyny, homophobia, and transphobia. From T. D. Jakes and Creflo Dollar to Bishop Eddie Long and Tony Evans, well-known Black southern ministers believe that "the breakdown of the family is the single greatest challenge that we face today," and that sexual immorality (out of wedlock sex, homosexuality, etc.) is its cause.[12] On the other hand, ministers participating in Moral Mondays, a movement that began April 2013 in North Carolina, have taken a different approach. These heterosexual or asexual leaders offer allyship in assessing broader political spheres and the impact of policy on many southerners' lives. These ministers regard civil disobedience as a moral duty, and they deploy it to protest conservative religious and Republican policies relating to voting rights, education, the environment, and healthcare. As a Moral Mondays document explains: "From the moral framework of the scriptures and our constitution we are calling together a coalition of goodwill, a nonviolent volunteer army of love, to oppose this legislature's heartless, ideologically driven agenda .... We call on all residents of North Carolina who believe in the common good to pray and partner with us as we use the tools of protest and the tactics of nonviolent moral suasion to illuminate for the nation the shameful acts taking place here."[13] Barber wants to utilize an approach that produced some positive results in the 1960s.

At various times, Moral Mondays participants have fought against legislation that negatively impacts the poor, women, and sexual minorities. They have not shied away from opposing targeted regulation of abortion providers or the HB2 bill, a.k.a. the bathroom bill, emphasizing the latter as a hate bill that violated civil rights. The Moral Mondays movement constitutes a strong aboveground movement. Nevertheless, the focus on moral consciousness in such movements assumes that we are simply in an imperfect democracy, as opposed to a dystopia. The South remains a sexual dystopia, and in that sense a moral revival alone will not help gender and sexual minorities. For example, long before HB2 and current attacks on Planned Parenthood in the South, Black communities were dealing with an HIV/AIDS crisis and poor women of all races reliant upon state assistance were being judged for nonheteronormative sexualities.

As Cathy Cohen's *Boundaries of Blackness* outlined years ago, Black communities' attention to the AIDS crisis was shaped by settler colonial approaches to sexuality and moral consciousness. Most recently, religious studies scholars have held Black church leaders accountable. Theology scholar Linda Thomas insists that "In the United States, who 'lives long and prospers' is indelibly linked to race, class, gender, and sexual orientation .... And how do religious collectives such as black megachurches respond to this dilemma?"[14] According to political scientist Eric L. McDaniel, the question has been answered: "The black church was forced to confront sexuality when gay marriage entered the political discourse .... Many historically black denominations, including AME, NBC, and the Church of God in Christ, passed resolutions or made statements that prohibited their clergy from officiating same sex marriages."[15] Despite all that has been accomplished by the Moral Mondays movement, the tactic of reviving moral frameworks said to exist in the country's founding documents and in optimistic interpretations of religious texts cannot alleviate hateful policies and violence that harm and kill vulnerable people, specifically gender and sexual minorities.

BY THE POWER VESTED IN ME: MORAL AUTHORITY, A PARODY OF HUMAN EMPATHY

The institution of marriage, and defense of it, remains an exemplary case of how limited calls for moral consciousness can be when applied to lives and beings not typically authorized by a moral authority, especially as it relates to intimate practices and family relationships. Only in a country majority-governed by the descendants of thieving people who constructed two documents, the Constitution of the United States and the Declaration of Independence, to overwrite and wipe out existing Indigenous laws, systems of gender, sexuality, and modes of socialization, while simultaneously enslaving a group of stolen people from another continent and converting them to religions that overwrote and erased their systems of gender, sexuality, and language would create a document that signals, nay proclaims, the very war and process of sexual imperialism and colonization they continue to deny: the Defense of Marriage Act. DOMA is a proclamation of a sex war. Bob Barr, a Republican representative from Georgia, authored the bill, H.R. 3396, and introduced it to the House of Representatives on May 1996. Former president Clinton signed it, turning another problematic bill into law. This one signaling a belief that marriage should be reserved for one man and one woma[n] that accompanied DOMA declared tha[t] upholding traditional morality, encouraging procreation in the context of families, encouraging heterosexuality—these and other important legitimate governmental purposes would be undermined by forcing another State to recognize same-sex unions."[16] Throughout the document, "family" is highlighted as the reason for creating the act. In Section A, which purportedly "advances the government's interest in defending and nurturing the institution of traditional, heterosexual marriage," the document makes clear the connection between a successful democracy and stable family. In doing so, the bill relies on legal and moral language to authorize its homophobia: "Certainly no legislation can be supposed more wholesome and necessary in the founding of a free, self-governing commonwealth, ... than that which seeks to establish it on the basis of the idea of the family, as consisting in and springing from the union for life of one man and one woman in the holy state of matrimony; the sure foundation of all that is stable and noble in our civilization; the best guaranty of that reverent morality which is the source of all beneficent progress in social and political improvement."[17] The bill's authors later illustrate the detrimental logics of moral authority as tied to the biological survival of the human race: "There are, then, significant practical reasons why government affords preferential status to the institution of heterosexual marriage. These reasons—procreation and child-rearing—are in accord with nature and hence have a moral component."[18] This section was ruled unconstitutional since it violated due process as outlined in the Fifth Amendment: "No person shall ... be deprived of life, liberty, or property, without due process of law." The Supreme Court overturned DOMA in 2015. However, before DOMA was overturned in 2015, marriage equality become a politically divisive ballot issue in many southern states.

When North Carolina was attempting to pass Amendment 1, Reverend Barber, acting in his capacity as president of the North Carolina chapter of the NCAAP, gave a speech at College Park Baptist Church in Greensboro, saying, "A vote on this so-called same-sex marriage amendment has nothing to do with your personal or religious opinion on same-sex marriage, but it has everything to do with whether or not you believe discrimination should be codified and legalized constitutionally .... whether you believe if hate should be legalized constitutionally."[19] Barber answers the previous question posed by this text: Does moral authority read and if so, what texts? In each case, Reverend Barber uses verses from the Bible, in addition to excerpts from the Constitution and the Declaration of Independence, to address the organization's main concern. The problem is that each of the documents utilized by Moral Mondays has also been used for creating the inequalities that exist. The contradictions arising from an inability to separate church from state cannot be ignored when dealing with the intersection of race with gender and sexuality. That Barber emphasizes the bill as steeped in hatred and as unconstitutional does not resolve the contradiction of morality and religion that he progressively politicizes. The amendment was approved but later overturned. However, these defeats have done little to quell the mounting use of religious freedom acts to spread hatred on the basis of gender and sexuality. We cannot ignore the role that moral authority plays in facilitating discrimination while also performing justification, progressiveness, and protection.

Discrimination is defined as the unjust or prejudicial treatment of different categories of people or things, especially on the grounds of race, age, or sex. While this definition sets up the precedents to pursue legal action, the value judgment of "unjust" is most often decided upon by those deemed to be the moral authorities. Hate crimes legislation seldom showcases the ways in which southern legislators continue to enact state violence via religious freedom acts without any threat of legal consequences. Such is the case when we examine the Marriage and Constitution Restoration Act from South Carolina: "To amend the code of laws of South Carolina, 1976, by adding Section 20–1–110 so as to enact the "Marriage and Constitution Restoration Act"; to define certain terms, including "parody marriage" and "marriage"; to provide that parody marriage policies are nonsecular in nature; to prohibit the state from respecting, endorsing, or recognizing any parody marriage policy or policies that treat sexual orientation as a suspect class; and for other purposes."[20] Not unlike DOMA, the bill seeks to define marriage as solely between one man and one woman, and to define anything outside of that as a parody marriage. However, the language within the bill not only lacks neutrality, but also, in its word choice (*parody* and *suspect*) devalues not simply the act of homonormative marriage but the persons pursuing the act. Parody, a term most readily associated with aesthetics and form in literary and performance art, denotes an imitation mode meant to signify comic effect or ridicule. Likewise, the phrase "suspect class" criminalizes individuals on the basis of sexual orientation. The hate that is spewed within this bill impacts the health and welfare of LGBTQ people, particularly aging LGBTQ couples, and any children who might find loving homes with LGBTQ parents. These are the rules of government and democracy that LGBTQ persons are navigating when seeking to be pronounced as human by those vested with power (moral authorities).

The call for a larger moral movement attempts to access unconditional citizenship and to claim a human project that is falsely touted as universal and extended to all. How does misunderstanding, ignorance, or hate of some people's gender, sex, or sexual orientation go undetected or become deeply embedded and absorbed within the ideologies and narrative of moral authority? The answer is two-prong. First, such elements are dressed and draped in aesthetics that convey rationalization (discursive practices) and spiritual depth (parables of fall and salvation): the law and the Bible. Second, these same aesthetics misdirect any attention away from power and the pursuit of it. That is, moral authority is itself a form of power bestowed to an institution or individual. In order to have moral authority over someone, or over a group or nation, said entity has to be deemed superior to that individual, group, institution, or nation. Enter settler colonialism.

According to Alicia Cox, "settler colonialism is an ongoing system of power that perpetuates the genocide and repression of indigenous peoples and cultures.... Settler colonialism normalizes the continuous settler occupation, exploiting lands and resources to which indigenous peoples have genealogical relationships. Settler colonialism includes interlocking forms of oppression, including racism, white supremacy, heteropatriarchy, and capitalism. This is because settler colonizers are Eurocentric and assume that European values with respect to ethnicity, and therefore moral superiority are inevitable and natural."[21] Native and African American studies scholars have noted how modes of assimilation, specifically the practice of chattel slavery, impacted the "Five Civilized Tribes" and their constructions of gender and sexuality, explaining that, "by relying on the coerced labor of enslaved men and women, Indian slaveholders, both male and female, redrew the parameters of their gender identities and the gendered division of labor."[22]

While this author does not believe the preservation of marriage is a life or death issue, it does remain an institution doing very contradictory work. Marriage does nothing to change the formation of moral authority that makes possible the destruction of families, countries, and entire societies. Marriage does nothing to ensure racial, gender, class, or sexual equality. Fighting for marriage equality, then, remains a very serious and problematic way to gain recognition of one's value in society and in the human race, as well as to access class privileges. When the preservation of white heteronormative patriarchy and the purity of white femininity served as the basis of a young country's national identity, Black, Native, and ethnic immigrants endured sexual violence, containment of their intimate relations and reproductive freedoms with regards to free or slave status, and control over who they could love as a result of miscegenation laws. Marriage, as it has been constituted in much of North America has been, and always will be, a colonial practice sustained by missionaries and religious conversion, Black Codes and Jim Crow, biopolitical terrorism, and gender and sexual violence. Understood in this context, communities or groups of people cannot be said to parody this practice, as the definition of parody hinges on comic effect, ridicule, or feebleness. Attempting to access the privileges of heteronormativity, citizenship, and civility without acknowledging the dystopia created by the defense of an unchanged institution means becoming colonizers and oppressors. In remembering what Indigenous and formerly enslaved groups endured as forced reproduction for labor, or as targets of miscegenation laws, we must also acknowledge that the compulsion to assimilate into European marriage institutions under the threat of state violence or collective homophobia and transphobia has been a failed attempt to live and to make living in the colonies bearable. Given these perspectives, then, might the slow tongue continue to be a useful alternative approach to settler colonialism's reliance upon moral authority?

Cultural producers have the power to do more than be vested with permission or made human by someone with power from a religious order. If the necessary work of Moral Mondays is to impact those who are not heteronormative and cisgender, then a comprehension of that moral consciousness has to be developed, fed, and grown using many different texts written by various authors, to avoid the pitfall of moral superiority. Moral consciousness shifts based on what literacies and forms of knowledge are used to feed the consciousness. If the Bible and the founding documents of imperial nations are the only texts from which to form a moral consciousness, then those most harmed by white supremacist heteropatriarchy will continue to be oppressed. Alternative texts from which to learn from need to be created and used. If the Moral Mondays' public policy framework, declared in its "Higher Ground Moral Declaration," is to be an effective counter to a neoconservative guard that also understands itself as doing the same work, there must be a real oppositional choice that can destabilize moral grounds.[23] Again, Cohen provides a useful alternative: "a politics where the *nonnormative* and *marginal* position of punks, bulldaggers, and welfare queens, for example, is the basis for progressive transformative coalition work."[24]

Influenced by Millie Jackson, the remainder of *A Dirty South Manifesto* addresses sexual resistance in the New South by chopping and screwing logics of moral authority that dictate much of southern life while highlighting alternative literacy practices about gender and sexuality. As with Millie Jackson's remake of Merle Haggard's song, some manifestos slow down themes of gender, race, and sexuality to a smooth, slow, stroking R & B beat to aesthetically chop and screw queer theory, settler colonialism, intersectionality, transstudies, and southern history and culture. In another of the manifestos presented here, readers may find that I have updated the husky authorial voice and southern cadence with a masterful literary southern drawl of femme militancy from hip-hop to produce a rhetorical slow tongue centered on taste and sensation. A couple of the manifestos strategically utilize satire and comedy before taking up the serious politics of sex. Finally, some of these manifestos and chapters work like Jackson's concept album, so that readers must account for multiple perspectives of marginalized groups on one subject. In the end, the most important lesson of the slow tongue insists upon language, performance, and discursive practices steeped in empathy and compassion as opposed to an order of moral authority. The problem with social policies' implicit use of colonial language practices is that their narrator/author remains an untrustworthy moral authority. In the next chapter, I examine how cultural creators, those without access to a narrative of moral authority and the pursuit of salvation, function as elements/nutrients/fertilizer of something that exists alongside moral consciousness. These persons create new texts from which to critique policy and make obvious the limitations of moral authority in contemporary social liberation movements centered on sexuality and gender.

Dirt Manifesto

Discussion of sexual resistance in the Old South, the New South, the Nuevo South, the Gulf South, the Deep South, the Border South, the South Atlantic, and any Souths that might pop up in the future should begin with sifting elements of the land. Dirt, specifically. Why? First, an intimate or spiritual relationship with land beyond ownership matters for sexual resistance. With the preservation of the land and earth in mind, sensual and erotic relationship with the land intervenes on the capitalist parsing of it for property; be it gentrification, loitering laws, or antiprostitution zones. Second, because geophagiaists have already determined that taste helps determine the quality of dirt, we have evidence that dirt can activate a sensorial compass that provides direction for what is not perceptible to the naked eye. There are things you can do in and with dirt that will ensure human survival. Embodied knowledge that could provide answers to questions relevant to indigeneity, colonization, displacement, and dispersal.

You have to want to get in the dirt. From there, accept what getting dirty means for you as opposed to someone else. Are you someone who can walk barefoot in it? Can you make a solid mud pie from it? Are you a person who requires tarp or blanket to sit on (top) of it? Do you need gloves to keep dirt from getting under your nails, or clothing to keep dirt-to-skin contact to a minimum? Whatever the answers, never fear getting dirty. Use dirt for what it was originally meant for: to grow a thing. Discern which seeds or crops can be planted in bad soil—dirt. A visual inspection might tell you if the soil is good or bad, but you might also have to touch it, smell it, or taste it to know.

Because it does not usually contain nutrients to grow, some horticulturalists say dirt is not soil. That dirt is dead soil. More recently and accurately, "they" suggest dirt is displaced soil: "And dirt? It's a group of runaways or kidnapped individuals that can't easily be associated with where they were born and grew up. In a sense, they're particles that have been rendered anonymous."[1] You mean like Africans, Natives, and the poor? Dirt's very existence is about dispossession and dispersal. Nevertheless, displaced soil, i.e. dirt, can be revitalized through vermicomposting—the use of red worms who feed off any organic matter and shit in the dirt, delivering important nutrients. These hermaphroditic red worms have five hearts, they have a reciprocal relationship with the land. They comprise a belowground movement; a species making the ground fertile for new living things. Since vermicomposting works, then dirt simply awaits its reanimation. The reanimators of dirt must have heart and many genders.

Be the red worm in the dirt . . . . Be the honeysuckle on the vine.

Use dirt to produce something other than nourishment and food, and reflect upon its uses as sustainable shelter. Dirt pro-

---

1. Janet Raloff, "Dirt Is Not Soil," *Science News,* July 27, 2008, https://www.sciencenews.org/blog/science-public/dirt-not-soil.

vides building material for natural and environmentally friendly architecture. Dirt, in the hands of any artist, becomes tool, ingredient, or craft material. Build cultural institutions out of dirt. In the hands of Wiccan, Hoodoo, and Voodoo witches, dirt from various places can be an ingredient for spells and powerful magic because it is a conductor of sacred energy. Create medicine from dirt. Build healing institutions out of dirt

If you don't use dirt as you would soil, to grow new life, then might you use dirt to sustain existing life, to cast spells, to save the environment, or to build what does not exist? Remembering that the South is populated with people and traditions traced to gods of earth, as well as people who believe in one god in the sky, the adage of sex as dirt(y) ceases to be sex as sin, secular, and evil.

CHAPTER TWO

What made you the way you are?
She'd say straight-faced it was
    the dirt she ate.
        Minnie Bruce Pratt, "Eating Clay"

....and obscenity is catching
    Audre Lorde, "JESSEHELMS"

The protest served to challenge Americans to
reconsider what objects they consider obscene,
normal, and acceptable in their daily lives.
    Jessica Jin, "Cocks Not Glocks" organizer

The exploitation of people in the United States may occur on
the basis of race and nation, but it also occurs with regards to
gender, class, and sexuality as a result of religious institutions
and governing systems imported onto stolen land to control
what is done with the land and with Indigenous people occupy-
ing the land. Existing spiritual metaphysics created from a non-
anthropocentric relationship to land, as well as their modes of
knowledge production, before the cosmic larceny was initiated,
are then displaced. Geophagia is the practice of eating dirt, soil,
or clay, "and is not uncommon in southern parts of the United
States as well as urban Africa," though "the American Psychiatric
Association defines [it] as persistent eating of nonnutritive

substances that is inappropriate to developmental level, occurs outside culturally sanctioned practice .... Where poverty and famine are implicated, earth may serve as an appetite suppressant and filler .... However, geophagia is often observed in the absence of hunger, and environmental and cultural contexts of the habit have been emphasized."[1] Eating dirt is an embodied practice that existed before medical boards and cartography and the treatments and treaties constructed out of them. Yet, compelled by the land's refusal to be metaphysically alienated from flesh, these dirt eaters pass on knowledge and minerals about an older system so that their descendants may know something more about the world than what dated treaties, proclamations, and certified disorders can tell them.

Though economically empowered white communities arduously invent religions or national identities out of opposing dirt, as well as create industry out of possessing it, when Black and Indigenous peoples, or poor queer whites, insist with effortless sensorial action upon the value, worth, and natural connection of dirt to living beings, it become geophagia, an illness or crisis to be healed or overcome.[2] Nevertheless, what dirt tastes like or the sensation that it evokes, gustatory perception and pleasure, is not what settler colonialism has alluded to in its articulation of geophagia as a mental disorder. William Schmidt, a *Times* reporter, recorded that southerner Fannie Glass asserted, "When it's good and dug from the right place, dirt has a fine sour taste." Glass later continues, "After a rainfall, when the earth smells so rich and damp and flavorful," is when she misses the practice.[3] Eating dirt denotes a particular relationship with the earth, one which cannot be understood in the context of settler colonialism, dispersion, and dispossession. In that same vein, gender and sexual fluidity cannot be understood within the systems of government established by settler colonialism: sexuality, in opposition to reproduction, has been articulated as dirty and gender as biologically fixed, with both being denounced as more flesh than spirit in dominant southern religious practices.

In this chapter, I rely upon my metaphorical use of dirt as sex in the Dirt Manifesto to think through imaginative transnational, diasporic, and Indigenous sexuality, eroticism, embodiment, sensorium, and intimacy practices that have been rendered immoral, anonymous, or displaced. Not unlike dirt as displaced soil, they must be revitalized by red worms. Embodied knowledge that is regional and cultural, such as the practice of eating dirt, reminds us that we must interrupt assimilationist practices like the enforced ideological split of body from mind or flesh from spirit. I argue that language and culture provide literacy practices that enable a different relationship to flesh, the body, or dirt, one in which alternative exchanges of ideologies about bodies and desires revitalize voices and movements for sexual resistance in the Dirty South. This chapter underscores obscenity as tactical response to the willful denial and alteration of spiritual systems and arrangements of family by setter colonialism, spiritual colonialism, and slavery. When displaced people are no longer on home soil, language and literacy practices become dirt awaiting animation from composting red worms. Words, like terra particles separated from their original source are kicked around, dug up, tilled, wind spattered across spaces to create new roads and paths, fertilized to produce soil just as valuable as roots of rich homelands.

The Dirt Manifesto also addresses the labor entailed in making dirt useful, and the risk entailed in being out of place. At this time, as in the past, radical southerners understand moral authority as an obstacle to overcome, risk being called obscene, and see what happens. Throughout this chapter, I examine what it means to be southerners on new ground influenced by a thesis of dirt and dirtiness. The Dirty South promotes nonanthropocentricism as part of its regional identity politics. Seemingly disparate issues demonstrate why strategies from the Dirty South signify the most cogent and vital ways to address homophobia, transphobia, and femme phobia in the evolving New South. Lesbians of color and their white allies in the post-Civil Rights era of literary activism, like contemporary feminist activists of U.S. college anti-campus carry campaigns, compel us to understand the ways in which queer women and nonbinary people demand more from traditional public spheres beholden to antiquated reliance upon moral authority in conservative church traditions. They create and provide cultural spaces of refuge and fugitivity to sustain people confronted with everyday gender and sexual violence because their gender or sexual orientation has not been authorized by moral leaders. Each example discussed throughout this chapter demonstrates why sexual resistance should continue to incorporate strategies of financially supporting the arts and humanities in the New South as much as one supports local churches.

In the *Black Manifesto*, Forman provided another provocative suggestion: "Black workers, black women, black students and the black unemployed are encouraged to seize the offices, telephones, and printing apparatus of all church sponsored agencies and to hold these in trusteeship until our demands are met."[4] Toward the end of the long twentieth century, lesbians found ways to do something akin to what Forman demands. In her spectacular historical study, *The Lesbian South: Southern Feminists, the Women in Print Movement, and the Queer Literary Canon*, Jamie Harker eloquently traces the broad overview of the women in print movement and lesbian imagination. Not unlike Kitchen Table Press in the Northeast, lesbian journals, presses, and social spaces such as *Sinister Wisdom, Feminary, Womon Writes, Woman News,* Woman Books, Naiad Press, Wild Iris Bookstores, and Charis Bookstores disrupted the dominance of moral authority in southern churches by providing women with a way to maintain their sense of worth and imagine new possibilities.

As Harker explained, "Struggling against the implicit racism, classism, and small-mindedness of their southern inheritance was a quixotic and generative gesture; the archive of southern lesbian feminism was invested in creating a South that was radical, queer, and free."[5] Lesbian presses, publishers, and community outlets in rural and metropolitan southern cities became nourishment for a consciousness that might thwart the immediate dangers of moral authority. Harker discusses notable authors of the era, the publishing politics of the era, differences being made between literary fiction and pulp/trash fiction with regards to publishers, as well as personal networks and friendships. Though Harker certainly broaches the intersections of women of color in the women in print movement and its successful era of lesbian publishing with her examination of Pat Parker, Alice Walker, and Ann Allen Shockley, this chapter provides a more concise examination of race, lesbian print culture, and moral authority by linking participants with other belowground cultural movements and aboveground political movements.

THE DIRT SHE ATE

Sinister Wisdom, the phenomenal and long-running multicultural, lesbian literary and arts journal, provides the first example of lesbian feminist resistance to moral authority frameworks in cultural production. After years of feeling isolated from lesbian and feminist communities while living in Charlotte, North Carolina, Catherine Nicholson and Harriet Desmoines decided to publish a lesbian feminist journal that could answer two questions: "How to think that keenly and imaginatively, how to develop that consciousness?"[6] As implied in the journal's title, they provided an answer to both questions by eschewing any calls for moral consciousness and moral authority, saying in the very first issue, "The consciousness we want *Sinister Wisdom* to express is ... lesbian or lunatic who embraces her boundary/criminal status, with the aim of creating a new species in a new time/space."[7]

Intent on distinguishing their publication from other lesbian journals at the time, Nicholson and Desmoines deliberately sought out contributions from women of color and refused a hierarchy between low and high culture in their issues. In the first issue, they acknowledged a notable absence and sent a plea for the next issue: "A central part of our vision has been to exercise the unconscious and therefore most deadly forms of racism in the feminist movement .... We need material from Third World women, especially Third World lesbians. We can't do what we set out to do without it."[8] The plea worked: Caribbean writer Michelle Cliff joined Adrienne Rich in editing the journal after Nicholson and Desmoines sold it upon moving from North Carolina in 1978. For two years, the South was their publishing headquarters. The region shaped their vision of what a lesbian imagination could do for all women.

Though no longer in the South, the journal continues to embrace its southern, antiracist roots. Most recently, *Sinister Wisdom* put out four special issues on lesbians in the South that demonstrated the intellectual, spiritual, cultural, and activist work that lesbians in the South have been doing for decades: "Lesbianima Rising: Feminist Arts in the South, 1974–96," "Landykes of the South," "Southern Lesbian Herstory 1968–94," and "Hot Spots: Creating Lesbian Space in the South." These issues were guest edited by a number of activists and culture makers. Journal editor Julie Enzer did an excellent job of using the special issues to bring attention to an important ongoing archival effort, the Southern Lesbian Feminist Activist Herstory Project (SLFAHP), initiated by the collective Womonwrites. In highlighting SLFAHP, Enzer has shown what lesbian feminist solidarity across state lines can look like.

As the guest editors of the "Hot Spots" special issue, Barbara Esrig, Kate Ellison, Merril Mushroom, and Rose Norman outlined the stakes of their issue: "In this twenty-first century, as lesbianism has become more commonplace, we need our strength in numbers more than ever. As danger and difficulty diminish, so do the triumphs and rewards of overcoming adversity .... Just as lesbian identity has been disappearing, diluted by the alphabet soup of non-traditional gender identity and expression, so are we losing lesbian space, lesbian community—both rare and very precious."[9] The editors speak nostalgically about lesbian separatism, and their sentiment echoes a chorus of contemporary lesbian voices dismayed by the publicness and activism around queer and trans identity politics that seemingly sublimate the oppression that many lesbians still endure. Yet, given *Sinister Wisdom's* founding mission of confronting racism and broadening definitions of who constitutes a lesbian audience, as explained in the journal's first issue, I want to trouble their statement. While lesbian separatism was an indispensable priority for the growth of lesbian presses early on, radical feminist and trans solidarity is necessity now in the dystopic South. When such fears are written by four cisgender white women, we might ask how race and class shape them. In the context of settler colonial sexuality, it becomes important to understand what is being lost and why it is being lost: white supremacist and capitalist heteropatriarchy. Reconsidering "Who Is Lesbian?" an essay in the first issue of *Sinister Wisdom,* with new solidarities in mind, Desmoines's words matter, "Not all the women who subscribe are lesbians, we don't think that makes this any less a journal devoted to the creation of a lesbian imagination. And we do think that creating a specifically lesbian imagination in politics and art is the most important gift any woman can give to all women, whether it's recognized as a gift or not. A consciously radical lesbian is a radical feminist with 'oomph.' The consistence of her politics does NOT make her morally superior, but it does give her freedom to imagine and freedom to lead."[10] By contrast, the previous statement from the guest editors of "Hot Spots" incorporates a sense of moral authority about gender that impacts lesbian, queer, and transgender coalitions, since it forecloses the possibility of lesbian imagination for trans and nongender-conforming communities. While Desmoines may have been referencing the heterosexual/homosexual binary, her words are still relevant for how to imagine coalitions between transwomen, transmen, and cisgender women. Feminist politics combined with lesbian imagination are important to securing and sustaining such coalitions and transfeminist practices. Lesbian identity appears overwritten by the politicization of fluid genders, but the function of white supremacy in the moniker could also impact lesbian identity. If the work around race and indigeneity from previous decades had continued, perhaps the erasure and invisibility of cisgender lesbianism might be less of a concern. An antiracist, lesbian imagination was crucial to gender and sexual resistance in the South then and remains so for the present and future.

Building off a combination of grassroots political organizing and the women in print movement, especially the contributions of Kitchen Table Press, the mid to late 1990s proved to be a significant time for women of color in print. In 1995, Charlene Cothran, then a lesbian and Black activist living in Atlanta, founded *Venus* magazine, a lifestyle magazine for Black lesbians. Named after her friend Venus Landian, a Black lesbian activist who died as a result of domestic violence in 1993, *Venus* enjoyed a subscription rate of over thirty-five thousand Black gay and lesbian readers. A few years later, a greater cultural boom emerged out of Atlanta— Redbone Press: "Founded in 1997 by Lisa C. Moore, Redbone Press corrected the dearth of Black lesbian voices in lesbian feminist publishing. Moore began researching the histories of feminist presses in 1995 while collecting and editing material for Redbone Press' first book, *Does Your Mama Know? An Anthology of Black Lesbian Coming Out Stories*."[11] Years later and now located in Washington, DC, Redbone Press continues to publish work celebrating the lives and experiences of Black gay and lesbians across generations. Moore's success has meant that she could explore new ventures with other like-minded folk, such as cofounding and co-organizing one of the most significant Black writers festivals in the twenty-first century, Fire and Ink. As the president of the festival organizing committee, Moore, along with vice president Steven Fullwood, ensured that Fire and Ink would also be an advocacy group for GLBT writers throughout the African diaspora.

Despite the women in press movement, and the inroads made by Cothran and Moore, the dominance of moral authority in the South was made especially clear when Cothran abruptly changed the mission of her much-adored magazine. In this case, the power of a lesbian imagination was not enough to erase the impact of weighty ideologies from Black Christian fundamentalism. Thirteen years after she founded *Venus* magazine, Cothran made a surprising announcement via her self-authored piece in the magazine, entitled "Redeemed! 10 Ways to Get Out of the Gay Life, If You Want Out": "As the publisher of a 13 year old periodical which targets Black gays and lesbians, I have had the opportunity to publicly address thousands, influencing closeted people to 'come out' and stand up for themselves .... But now, I must come out of the closet again. I have recently experienced the power of change that came over me once I completely surrendered to the teachings of Jesus Christ. As a believer of the word of God, I fully accept and have always known that same-sex relationships are not what God intended for us."[12] She would go on to publicize a new mission for the magazine, insisting that it would continue to "encourage, educate and assist those who desire to leave a life of homosexuality." Though such sentiments may seem antiquated and analog in a digital era of sexual identity, the belief in a moral authority and the rhetoric of fallen and redeemed man continues to be influential, as witnessed by the rise in advocacy for reparative therapy/conversion therapy and the formation of the ex-gay movement. Each of these combined shame and stigma into a pseudo health/medical movement. The betrayal and death of *Venus* magazine underlines why more must be done to excavate the histories of sexual resistance in the South, in addition to celebrating their futurity.

OBSCENITY IS CATCHING

While Black women in the South did not necessarily take control of printing apparatuses in churches, as Forman suggested, they did understand community models of printing and writing as valuable in their daily lives in a way that a history of women in print movement cannot fully capture. They understood that telling their stories was simply a first step. Here, I briefly link Black women writers affiliated with the women in print movement to colleges and universities, as well as community institutions of higher learning, to understand why writing and teaching provided a significant second step in gender and sexual resistance: the production of new knowledge helps counter the dominant narrative of a singular moral authority. Audre Lorde and Ann Allen Shockley provide examples of writing and teaching that interrupt certain southern essentialisms, since, as Harker notes, "the archive of southern lesbian feminism created alternative myths to counteract the 'enhanced but essential South' of an emerging southern literature."[13] Considering modes of writing that are intergenerational, lesbian, immigrant, and less commercial alongside strategies of teaching and learning in educational institutions provides an alternative overview about the relationship among dirt, creativity, and imagination than the one offered by the women in print movement.

Writer and community educator Alexis Pauline Gumbs's courses centered on Audre Lorde have demonstrated how cultural geographies of the South remain underdiscussed elements in Lorde's writings. Like Gumbs, we must make the connections, for those who will not, between a Caribbean-immigrant consciousness transplanted into the tumultuous land and politics of the Old and Deep South. As *I Am Your Sister: Collected and Unpublished Writings of Audre Lorde* lays out, Lorde had a connection to Spelman College in Atlanta that led to the archiving of her papers there in 1995. Lorde's close ties to Ruby Sales, Beverly Guy-Sheftall, and Johnnetta Cole at Spelman College were part of the reason she moved beyond some negative experiences she had in the South with regards to race and sexuality. Yet, well before leaving her papers to Spelman, Lorde forged commitments to shaping southern Black body politics in ways that would foreshadow her imprint on the Dirty South.

In 1968, Audre Lorde was a writer-in-residence at Tougaloo College in Jackson, Mississippi. During that time, she provided and participated in writing workshops with African American students at the historically Black college. As Alexis DeVeaux found, Lorde was initially unsure of how to go about being a teacher-poet. "When the poetry workshop convened, Lorde was terrified. She knew nothing about teaching poetry, and had little or no formal knowledge of poetic theory. Nor had she even been in this kind of relationship with black people before."[14] This experience alerted Lorde to how teaching writing could be an important contribution to movements against racism and sexism. She would explain to interviewer Claudia Tate that her time at Tougaloo was "pivotal" because, as she notes, "it was my first trip into the deep South; it was the first time I had been away from the children. It was the first time I dealt with young Black students in a workshop situation. I came to realize that this was my work, that teaching and writing were inextricably combined, and it was there that I knew what I wanted to do for the rest of my life."[15] With the help of Galen Williams, she would go on to publish Tougaloo students' work in a literary magazine entitled *Pound*. This was a major accomplishment, not only for the students but for Lorde. She would later teach at other universities and colleges: Lehman, CUNY, and Hunter. For Lorde, teaching was the production of new knowledge that could sustain a lesbian imagination threatened by the dominance of moral authority. She came to recognize it as a form of activism, alongside writing and protest. Her pedagogy practices on the page and in the classroom would obscenely challenge white supremacist heteropatriarchy.

During the last years of her life, Lorde's engagement with southern body politics and moral consciousness would inform the legacy she was leaving, specifically in the 1990s. When Lorde and Minnie Bruce Pratt won the 1990 creative writing fellowships from the National Endowment for the Arts (NEA), Jesse Helms referred to their poetry as obscene as part of his political attack on the NEA and funding protocols for public money. Helms had been elected to his first term as a U.S. senator from North Carolina in 1972. Helms, a five-term conservative Republican, was known for both failed and successful amendments related to abortion and obscenity. Helms's amendments were notable because of the ways in which they alternatively ignored and appealed to freedom of speech, while strategically laying the groundwork for censorship as a compromise that could protect legal rights and honor moral authority. One particular example involving Helms showcases the historical links between moral authority, moral consciousness, and sexual morality as being about settler sexuality. In 1988, the Southeastern Center for Contemporary Art came under fire for exhibiting visual artist Andres Serrano's "Piss Christ," which presented a crucifix submerged in urine. The piece infuriated Helms.

On July 26, 1989, Helms submitted Amendment 420 to introduce guidelines about NEA funding for obscene or offensive work, since the publicly funded NEA had awarded Serrano fifteen thousand dollars in prize money. Under this amendment, if a council board found materials to be obscene, the NEA was strongly advised to not fund the artist's application. Any works featuring homoeroticism, BDSM, or the exploitation of children fell under the rubric of obscene and indecent.[16] Before this incident, Helms had established policies steeped in a sexual morality that penalized the poor and LGBTQ populations in North Carolina.[17]

As a result of his attack on Lorde, as well as previous attacks on other artists of the time, Lorde would write and publish "JESSEHELMS," a poem with important lines for future generations to relish whenever their Helmsian figure(s) might emerge:

> I am a Black woman
> writing my way to the future
> off a garbage scow knit from moral fibre
> stuck together with jessehelms'
> come where Art is a dirty word
> scrawled on the wall of
> Bilbo's memorial outhouse[18]

Lorde demonstrates how deeply impacted she was by her time in the South when she aligns Helms's tactics to Theodore G. Bilbo, a notorious U.S. senator from Mississippi and Klansman whose statue resides in the Mississippi capitol building. Lorde's entire poem reminds readers that Helms's crusade against the NEA derived from an older tradition and philosophy—white supremacy, patriarchy, and imperialism held in place by a powerful foundation of moral authority.

RISK AND VULNERABILITY

Even if it means producing knowledge that colonizers would classify as obscene, Lorde's work makes it clear that art and universities must remain sites where we risk misunderstanding. Likewise, Ann Allen Shockley exemplifies the necessity of a lesbian imagination for marginalized and outcast persons living in the South, ever aware of the usefulness of southern discretion. *Loving Her, Say Jesus and Come to Me,* and *The Black and White of It* form Shockley's influential legacy. Though Shockley wrote when a Black feminist lesbian writers' movement was occurring, she remained a southern outlier who declined lesbian identity.[33] She also never classified herself within or against Black arts movements of the time.

Like Lorde, who also received a master's degree in library science, Shockley carved out a space in universities. She was an archivist, taught library science, and wrote fiction, all in the service of producing new knowledge about Black culture, Black women, and Black same-sex desire. She is responsible for important published scholarly works about Black librarianship and Black special collections in libraries. These decolonial approaches to library science are the understated foundations that make Black studies possible. Like the research and writing she did on African American special collections as a librarian for the Special Negro Collection at Fisk University, Shockley's fiction traversed into queerness as it is currently understood. Turning to Shockley's most recent novel, *Celebrating Hotchclaw* (2005), showcases how her careers as writer and librarian produce new knowledge about gender and sexuality that is attentive to regionalism and moral authority.

Celebrating Hotchclaw fictionally represents the moral codes that influence LGBTQ faculty and students and college life in the South's historically Black colleges and universities (HBCUs). In the novel, Professor Michael Elaine is involved in an accident that reveals that the professor, who identified as male, was legally assigned a female gender at birth. When one of the main characters, Laramie, who is an old college friend of Michael from their

Mount Holyoke days, goes to his apartment to help her hospitalized friend, she observes: "That was when she saw them: the neatly arranged men's clothes of trousers, coats, shoes. At a loss, she wondered if she had been given the key to the wrong apartment.... Then she saw the plastic Hotchclaw ID card. *Dr. Michael Stower, Assistant Professor. Male.*"[19] Shockley writes about Laramie's anxiety and fear of anyone else learning the secret, and what that would mean for her friend and for Hotchclaw University, which is celebrating its centennial year. As Shockley takes readers through the dull ordinariness of academic research and teaching, service committees, and home life, she highlights the structures of moral authority shaping modern Black HBCU college life, where lesbians may be acknowledged, though not fully accepted, and trans identity remains beyond the veil of comprehension. Moreover, because Laramie works at a historically white Penn Murray State, where she serves as director of the university's women's center, Shockley calls out the hypocrisy of feminist politics and leadership that could build a women's center while remaining wedded to binary, fixed models of gender.

Not unlike the early-twentieth-century passing novels about race and community, *Celebrating Hotchclaw* draws upon genre conventions of melodrama, sentimentality, and romance. Employing the plot device of the college's celebration of its history, Shockley uses the links between the histories of colleges and universities, slavery, and Reconstruction to think about the relationality between racial segregation and gender segregation in our contemporary era, in ways that bathroom bills cannot. The benevolence and patronage of white southerners is juxtaposed with the quest for public funding and external donations; each is shaped by agendas that have everything to do with sexual morality. When another character, Portia, the love interest of Michael, is depicted reading a letter by a descendant of one of the white founding fathers of Hotchclaw, the critique is clear: "As you are aware, I came here to help with the educating of the Negroes in the South. As a Christian, I felt it my duty to come; as a white man, my responsibility. I have fallen in love with a beautiful and intelligent Negro woman who teaches with me .... Since it is forbidden for races to intermarry in the South, I am declaring myself a Negro."[20] Though the histories of racial and gender passing are different and divergent, Shockley's use of them reveals how and why they sometimes intersect within institutions and their missions. The racial passing story that Portia uncovers in the archives foreshadows her own dilemma: whether her love of Michael will allow her to accept his gender. Shockley's attention to Christian influence among education missionaries remains important to contemporary sexual politics and HBCUs throughout the South. Past incidents of gender and sexual violence on U.S. college campuses compel us to understand the ways in which culture, sexual expression, and queerness produced by writers such as Lorde and Shockley demand more from traditional public spheres beholden to antiquated reliance upon moral authority in conservative church traditions. In recent years, several HBCUs have been celebrating their historic mission while also creating space for gender and sexual equity on college campuses.

In addition to Spelman College's initiatives and curriculum committee, Morehouse University recently changed its policy in order to accept transmen, though its admission policies appear unable to address gender fluidity, femmeness, and transitioning. Bowie State University was the first HBCU to create an LGBTQ center. Fayetteville State University and North Carolina Central University (NCCU) have LGBTQ equity centers. Tia Doxy, a straight ally and director of student life, explained why the creation of the center was important to the evolution of NCCU and its student population: "If students can't come to the classroom and be their authentic self, how can we give them hope to be successful .... These students demonstrate what courage looks like every day."[21] At NCCU, Doxey worked with faculty member David Jolly to serve as the first advisors for COLORSA (Creating Open Lives for Real Success), the LGBTQ student organization. Their efforts contributed to support and discussion that paved the way for an LGBTQ center opening in 2013. Doxy once explained, "It is not easy to be an ally.... You have to be willing to interrupt prejudice and discrimination knowing that the same discrimination that the LGBT community faces, you may also encounter." NCCU now hosts an annual Lavender Graduation ceremony. NCCU is also home to three other queer organizations: D.O.M.S., OutLaw, and Polychromes.[22] HBCUs are rarely located in isolated, "middle of nowhere" areas, and their links to and influence on broader Black and sexual marginalized communities must be highlighted as a key factor of sexual resistance in the Dirty South. Shockley does so throughout *Celebrating Hotchclaw* precisely because she recognizes new possibilities for a twenty-first century HBCU.

THE OBSCENITY OF VIOLENCE

While Lorde's time in the U.S. South was brief, her attention to obscenity crusades provides us with a transnational feminist lens with which to read contemporary queer public protests and the New South, or Nuevo South. Additionally, as Ann Allen Shockley's work demonstrated, colleges and universities must refuse a politics of respectability when issues of gender and sexuality

oppression are at stake. Both writers exemplify why the Cocks
Not Glocks campaign initiated by students at one university in
the Nuevo South chose obscenity and the setting of their college
campus to make a point about gun violence. In examining the
lived experiences of Latinas/os and Asians in Arkansas, Perla
Guerro writes, "the Nuevo South is the newest manifestation of
the New South—a regime built on white supremacy, the exploitation of racial difference, and increasingly, legal statuses such as
citizen, refugee, or undocumented immigrant that define the
experiences of new southerners."[23] The emphasis on the racialization of these groups shaped by specific regionalism also matters for gender and sexual resistance, especially for individuals
belonging to a racial group consistently typified as a model
minority. Outside of Arkansas, specific regionalisms around sexual morality intersected with racial and gender formations during August 2016, in the Cocks Not Glocks campaign at the University of Texas, Austin. The campaign has been described by its
creator and organizer, Jessica Jin, as fighting absurdity with
absurdity: "The event was satirically named 'Campus (Dildo)
Carry' to mock the new 'Campus Carry' law. It was created upon
the discovery that it is illegal, according to Texas obscenity laws,
to openly brandish a harmless dildo in public. In contrast, loaded
guns (concealed or otherwise) capable of inflicting instant death
are often legally welcomed and encouraged."[24] The operation is
creative and unique in its approach to bringing attention to the
campus carry law, which makes it legal to have a concealed hand-
gun on college campuses throughout Texas. In the 1980s, rallying
words spoken by Jin during the campaign might have had a different meaning: "Let's put a dildo in the hands of every pissed-off
college student who hasn't been heard yet in this safety conversation!"[25] Far from a rallying cry for self-determining sex or safe

sex to combat the Reagan-era increase in government funding for abstinence-only sexual education or mishandling of the AIDS epidemic, Jin's exuberant prose was meant to rally forces against open-carry, campus gun laws. Whereas Lorde counters attacks on her poetry with explicit sexual language and violent imagery to highlight the atrocity of homophobic and sexist politics and address censorship, Jin turns to obscenity and absurdity to address mass gun violence. The campaign spawned similar campaigns across college campuses in the United States, with chapters popping up in states such as Wisconsin.

Jin, the daughter of Chinese immigrants, was born in Tennessee and raised in San Antonio, Texas, and was heavily influenced by her parents' Republican politics and southern Christianity.[26] Jin once expressed how racialization impacts her life in Texas, and how her civil disobedience leadership challenged "model minority" stereotypes: "This protest came about and lots of people didn't expect it from an Asian American woman .... Perhaps the quiet and submissive stereotype is what made it easier for me to come out of nowhere and scare people."[27] Therefore, the tone and approach of her civil disobedience should not be misunderstood as frivolous. Though not articulated as explicitly antireligious, her mode of public protests represents Guerro's call to better understand the role religion plays in racial formation in anti-Black structures and anti-Black racism in the South.[28] The choice to utilize obscenity is a critique of the shifting and oppressive use of moral authority by white supremacist heteropatriarchy, whose history of violence has been repeatedly dismissed as the exercise of a constitutional right.

Jin's efforts successfully created more conversation about gun violence, but they also demonstrated why there must be more explicit and nuanced discussion of sexuality and sexual violence within the campaign and in movements about sexual resistance in general. After Jin's graduation, her work was taken up by another woman of color and UT student, Ana López, the child of Mexican immigrants from Austin.[29] When we contextualize the efforts of these two children of immigrants with Guerro's words and alongside the legacy of feminists such as Celine Parreñas Shimizu, Chandra Mohanty, Audre Lorde, or Gloria Anzaldúa, individuals who have theorized the power of the erotic, sex positivity, and transnational sexuality as a counter to representations of sexual morality, sexual violence, and dispossession in the colonized Americas, we better comprehend how and why their efforts exceeded the boundaries of heteronormative civil disobedience.

The campaign's absurdist conjoining of sex toys with guns signaled an unresolved issue concerning how any remnants of sexuality are made sinful and rendered in power plays in the United States. While the campaign's emphasis on fighting absurdity with absurdity was a brilliant cultural tactic for combating gun violence, opposing responses to it quickly showcased how white heteropatriarchy reinforces the conflation of sex with violence when a simultaneous full critique of sex negativity and sexual immorality is not already present in local politics and culture. A year or so after the campaign started, the necessity of greater discussion about settler sexuality's link with violence became obvious when Jin and others begin to experience online trolling that demonstrated the way sexuality and violence have always been linked in this society. As *Cosmopolitan* magazine reported, Jin had to file a police report as a result of receiving the following comment on her Facebook page: "#HaveEmAllShot stand up to these little *sluts* and be the American you must be."[30] The online bullying demonstrated how women's sexual autonomy and public voice are always seen as a threat to white male supremacist patriarchy. However, the eccentricity of the Cocks Not Glocks campaign initiates a conversation that was glossed over in responses to mass shootings such as those at the Pulse Nightclub, Parkland High School, or Santa Fe High School, as well as rejection shootings and those prompted by gay/trans panic—one that denies both masculine entitlement and the privileging of heterosexuality.[31] As the Cocks Not Glocks movement has evolved, Jin and others have insisted upon clearer delineations of how violence is linked to gender and sexual oppression and have provided multiple fronts to critique sexual terror and violence. We should follow their lead to better strategize around sexual violence.

According to reports, the University of Texas, Austin antigun carry campaign received more than forty-five hundred donated dildos from Hustler Hollywood and from HUM vibrators in Austin.[32] Optimistically, we could read these companies as offering support for the students' queer modes of protest. Cynically, this is an example of heteroeconomies that are opportunistic and neoliberal, co-opting political activism for publicity. Why doesn't the sexual freedom and sexual education of queer and transfolk elicit the same type of corporate support? Dildos may be perceived as symbolic of phalluses and a privileging of men, but they have also been useful in the sexual autonomy of gender fluid individuals, in the gender expressions of sexual desire and performance of lesbians and gay men, and in nonheteronormative sexual play for others. Beyond gun control, the dildo becomes a useful political prop for politics that fail to interrogate problematic narratives touting the danger of queer and trans sexuality. Since experts have insisted that sexual well-being is an important component of mental health, why are free dildos not a thing on every college campus even when guns are not involved? Women, queers, and transfolk too often lose their lives because societies conjoin cocks and glocks: toxic masculinity takes shape in sexual violence and state-sanctioned violence on marginalized communities, conveyed via homophobic and transphobic policies. These shootings are not only about gun laws, but also about how limited perspectives of sexuality and gender are shaped by moral narratives that devalue women as well as gender and sexual variation.

Gendered threats of violence against the creators of the campaign demonstrate the difficulty that a new generation will have in attempting to divorce sexuality from violence. For that delinking to happen it will take concerted efforts to reeducate citizens about gun culture alongside education about women's desire and sexual culture in order to interrupt the misogyny and eroticization of violence within global state agencies and social institutions. Changing the cultural conditions from which much of this violence arises, the eroticization of guns and the antierotic foundations of gender and sexual socialization, is how legislative change will happen in southern states.

In many ways, women cannot wait for religious institutions to wipe clean the debt they have burdened women with for centuries. For if the party line is that we are all born into sin, then only one gender seems to bear the burden/weight of this spiritual mark. Like Forman, then, I continue to advocate something that a moral revival will not do: reflecting upon the obscenity of settler sexuality and settler colonial politics and reveling in and rolling around in the dirt to make new knowledge about gender and sexuality. In addition to all the self-funded blogs/vlogs, webshows, and podcasts that use new technology to pursue the spread of a lesbian feminist imagination, there must be financial remuneration that goes to these sites, as well as to analog feminist organizations, institutions, schools, and universities.[33] These must be feminist-, as opposed to woman-led.

In addition to the need to support existing cultural institutions and build new ones, the support of universities, especially public universities, in their formation of women, gender, and sexuality studies programs is essential to remaining vigilant in countering the fallacy of moral authority. Though some critics would suggest that these institutions serve an elite and specific population, the presences of first-generation, queer, and racial minority students suggest that this is not always the case. In addition, the presence of such programs provides a way to ensure that history does not repeat itself. In 1960s Florida, LGBTQ students and faculty were rounded up in bar raids by local police and in college dorms by agents working for the notorious Johns Committee or Florida Legislative Investigative Committee. Like COINTELPRO, this agency took great strides to make sure that gay and lesbian educators who could corrupt young minds were barred from state institutions. From coercing suspected students into being spies to publishing the 1964 report "Homosexuality and Citizenship in Florida," the state sought to control and contain ideologies that could shift consciousness around sexuality and gender. Faculty and students at public universities endured enormous surveillance and policing during this time.[34] Such history underscores why recent public controversies over the defunding of women's studies and African American studies programs and departments matter for southern universities, both for the students and for the communities surrounding them. Liberatory education, as Paulo Friere noted, "makes sense because women and men learn that through learning they can make and remake themselves, because women and men are able to take responsibility for themselves as beings capable of knowing—of knowing that they know and knowing that they don't."[35] Universities, teachers, and students obscenely engaged in the practice of liberatory learning conceptualize ways out of and around moral authority for all.

Geophukit Manifesto

Geoph(aa)agia, Geophagia(ge), Geophagiii
There are erotics to southern mispronunciations arising
    from
a slow tongue trying to access a mother tongue.
Geophagia; how about geophuckit for when
Eshu, Coyote, Kokopelli, and Anansi
topple monuments of
Sam, Grant, Jefferson, and Robert,
throwing dust and yelling,
Geophuckit Muthafucka!
What is your relationship to the land?
Are you native, settler, or arrivant?
Geophagia; how about geophuckit?
Was your mama a WNIA member?
Did she know any of them muthfuckas on the Commission
    of Indian Affairs?
You got ancestors who wrote and benefitted from the Indian
    Trade and Intercourse Act(s)?

Then the Treaty of Guadalupe?

Did your ancestors enslave Africans in the transition from
  "barbaric" Native tribes to "Civilized" Nations?

Or John Marrant they Black asses down to the colonies
  preaching the devil is a liar to "natives"?

Geophagia ... how about geophuckit: What is the Dawes Act
  and its subsequent commissions?

Did your ancestors steal people, or hang Black bodies from
  trees?

Or just watch the ones that did?

Would you say that this practice constitutes a mental
  disorder, a symptom of poverty, a famine of some sort?

And do they matter to PETA as much as possums falling
  from the sky in Brasstown, NC ?

As much as colonists rowing themselves ashore mattered to
  Indigenous folk in North and South Americas, Africans
  in the Old World, or peace-treaty thefts at the Southwest
  borders?

As much as the Lumbees sexually resisting, generationally
  refusing the white logic of settlers?

Geophagia, how about geophuckit?

Geophuk that story about Adam, Eve, and creation myths
  that led to communion Sundays of wine drinking, cracker
  eating, or sacrament kneeling before god-praising
  pedophiles?

Would you say that practice constitutes a mental disorder, a
  symptom of poverty, a famine of some sort?

Geophukit Muthafuckas!

All day, everyday. Geophukit ... geophukit ... geophukit ...
  geophukit ... GEOPHUKIT!

CHAPTER THREE

My formulation of "southscape" engages, then, the
natural environment and the social collective that
shapes that environment out of its cultural beliefs,
practices, and technologies.

Thadious Davis, *Southscapes: Geographies of Race,
Region and Literature*

Who's willing to take the challenge or the risk to step
out there and see what happens?

Mandy Carter, "Interview with Author"

Did you not like our work with transgender women?
Did you not like that we speak out for the LGBT
community? Do you not like that we speak out for
women? Which one of those things is it?

Deon Haywood, WWAV, NOLA.Com

In the United States, dispossession and displacement have historically been discussed in reference to removal and tribal sovereignty or to slavery and reparations, since state allocations of
natural and economic resources have led to structural and systemic inequalities having to do with race and class. Yet, the issue
of land also inevitably intersects with how gender and sexuality
is regulated in the United States. Contemporary modes of terror
and violence visited upon sexual minoritarians too often mimic
histories of settler colonial violence demonstrated in the admin-

istration of Indian removal in 1830, slavery, Reconstruction-era rape and lynching law, or police raids on LGBTQ venues in the McCarthy era. The illusion of safe spaces under the presence of settler colonialism is created by ownership and possession of land, or by white identity. Moreover, the theft of land becomes the foundation from which governing documents can be created to overwrite preexisting understandings of land, law, nature, and the human. Land politics dictate how institutions can carry out their missions, determine which institutions are worth state and national advocacy, and which communities' experiences of culture are worthy of institutional curation. The formation of family and social networks, and the modes of intimacies within those institutional spaces, dictate land politics. Sexual morality, then, is undeniably a powerful factor in land politics that must be and has been resisted in the Dirty South.

Emphatically shaped by histories and cultural narratives within Native America and African America, the Geophukit Manifesto was inspired by Millie Jackson's "Phuk It Symphony" and written from a trickster's point of view of the land and sexually decolonized land politics. Influenced by Thadious Davis's concept of southscape, this chapter asks how local southern geopolitics influence gender and sexual resistance and imagination. It discusses the intersection of sexuality and gender with concerns of race and region through examinations of pornographers, lesbian activists and community developers, and sex workers and sex work activists. Specifically, it highlights how mobility as a tactic in sexual commerce and consumption, sexual identity politics and activism, and sexual labor practices can challenge heteronormative supremacist land politics as dictated by setter colonialism and setter sexuality. Beginning with a Fanonian-like discussion of decolonization and key terms from

Indigenous studies enables it to consider geographical nuances and race-conscious critiques of religious freedom acts and the foundation of moral authority that undergirds each.

Jodi Byrd uses the term "arrivant" to "signify those people forced into the Americas through the violence of European and Anglo-American colonialism and imperialism around the globe."[1] The Geophukit Manifesto is a Black manifesto crafted from the foundations of Black power and employing the perspective of an arrivant to do what Byrd later calls for when she, "asks that settler, native, and arrivant each acknowledge their own positions within empire and then reconceptualize space and history to make visible what imperialism and its resultant settler colonialisms and diasporas have sought to obscure."[2] The latter part of Byrd's request is why Forman's earlier critique of white Christian churches matters for this manifesto, and it also illuminates why the Dirty South critique of both sexual morality and work ethic is important to sexual resistance in the New South: because resistance must question and critique the deployment of practices from these colonial religious institutions in the everyday regulation of Indigenous and arrivant gender and sexuality today.

HETEROSEXUAL MONUMENTS: ADAM AND EVE'S FREEDOM OF EXPRESSION AND HETEROECONOMY

Sexual commerce in the form of pornography and sex toys has been a lucrative enterprise in the United States. Therefore, I turn to examine the ways in which sexual consumption practices of the "deviant sexual cultures" assumed to threaten heteronormativity have simply secured domestic heterosexuality's transformation into global heterosexual economies. According to Cathy Cohen, "an understanding of the ways in which heteronormativity works to support and reinforce institutional racism, patriarchy, and class exploitation must ... be a part of how we problematize current constructions of heterosexuality."[3] While Confederate monuments have garnered a great deal of attention in the last few years of white supremacist controversies, sites of memory predating the Civil War provide examples of how heteronormativity reinforces institutional racism, patriarchy, and class exploitation. In 1894, the Roanoke Colony Memorial Association purchased land on which to place a commissioned marker/monument to commemorate the arrival of the first colonists led by Sir Walter Raleigh in 1594. Known as the Virginia Dare Marker and placed on Roanoke Island, North Carolina, it reads, "Near this place was born, on the 18th of August, 1587./Virginia Dare./the first child of English parents born/in America .... Virginia Dare was baptized. Manteo, the/friendly chief of the Hatteras Indians/had been baptized on the Sunday preceding. These baptisms are the first/known celebrations of a Christian sacrament in the territory of the thirteen original United States."[4] Unsurprisingly, the marker does not contain the language around religious freedom that is found in the country's founding documents and that has been linked with contemporary white supremacist groups' mission rhetoric. The marker captures the discursive violence of settler colonialism and its link with not only racial but also sexual and gender terror via religious institutions. The stone marks the importance of European white reproductivity to the young nation's future; it also signals the overwriting of Indigenous spiritual practices and traditions with Christian sacrament. According to Scott Morgensen, "the imposition of colonial heteropatriarchy and the hegemony of settler sexuality" is that it "sought both the elimination of Indigenous sexuality and its incorporation into settler sexual modernity."[5] This has happened through settler colonial logics of moral authority as it relates to religious freedom and freedom of expression.

Having already explored how monogamous, heterosexual, intraracial marriage becomes a form of settler sexuality, I turn to a vastly different case study centered on the sex industry corporation PHE Inc., or Adam and Eve as it is more widely known, which sells pornographic videos, educational sex videos, and sex toys. In my reading of Adam and Eve, I demonstrate how moral authority sanctions heterosexual supremacy, while delimiting broader sexual resistance and freedom in the New South. Adam and Eve and its owner, Philip Harvey, have never been fully contextualized within the 1980s sex war debates in which figures such as Hugh Heffner and Larry Flynt battled against antiporn feminists and obscenity legislation. Yet, all three sex empires were made possible by the country's founding document, the U.S. Constitution, and its First Amendment, which invalidated existing Indigenous laws, modes of being, and evolving identities. Legal sexual industries are made possible not simply because they contribute to the liberties and freedoms of sex-positive Americans, but because the quest for and practice of such freedom is enacted by an everyday denial of what came before that version of sexuality: reproductive freedom, free sex, various expressions of sexuality and gender, pre-criminalized sexual bartering, sacred dildos, two-spirit beings, non-monogamous intimacy, and nonnuclear family structures.

Adam and Eve's corporate logo can be read as a southern flag or monument that attests to the historical making of heterosexuality and heterosexual marriage in modern Western empires.

The name of the company, Adam and Eve, is bracketed by a red apple symbol. Despite the queer and trans uses of pornographic magazines, videos, and sex toys, PHE publicly highlights, then defensively addresses, the queering that happens within sexual industries. As its website states under the "Career" tab: "PHE, Inc. is an employee-owned company based on a 10-acre site in historic Hillsborough, N.C.... one of the largest private employers in the county with a diverse staff of over 300 people, from recent high school and college graduates to white-haired grandparents."[6] In addition, the company profile highlights that it donates 20 percent of its earnings to the nonprofit DKT, whose focus is on population control, HIV prevention, reproductive health, and family planning in various international communities. Such statements and international philanthropic endeavors provide a company profile of ordinariness and goodness, as opposed to the seediness or sensationalist glitz associated with sex companies outside of the South. As Harvey recounts in *The Government vs. Erotica: The Siege of Adam and Eve*, the history of the company cannot be delinked from sexual commerce and heterosexual family: "Our mailing of sexually-oriented products began in 1970 with selling condoms by mail. I was working toward my Masters in Family Planning Administration in the School of Public Health at the University of North Carolina Chapel-Hill. As part of my thesis work, I obtained permission from the university to experiment with the mail order sale of condoms as part of an effort to find new ways of delivering contraceptives outside clinic-based networks."[7] The Population Planning Association (later PHE) began as a collaboration between Harvey and Tim Black, who were both committed to nonmedical family planning. They soon moved onto mailing "books and publications about contraception and reproductive physiology."[8] The business of family planning did not preclude the marketing of pleasure and eroticism in the state of North Carolina, specifically in Alamance and Orange Counties, not too far away from the University of North Carolina and Duke University. Their efforts to partially shift thinking about family planning occurred three years before obscenity was legally defined in *Miller v. California* (1973): however, as attorneys informed them, they were still legally liable under Comstock laws and could still be persecuted for obscenity if someone found out what they were doing. As seen elsewhere, the status of the university as site of new knowledge production cannot be disentangled from determining whether, in a given case, sexual morality's codes for gender and sexuality will play a role in U.S. imperialism. Here, public health, family planning, and sexual commerce emerge in legal conflict with nationalist ideologies but they do share a common goal—preservation of heteronormative families.

FAMILY PLANNING AND SETTLER COLONIALISM

Notably, long before Adam and Eve was headquartered in Hillsborough, Orange County was occupied by the Occaneechi of the Saponi Nation, who migrated to the area at the end of the 1600s as a result of violent removal conflicts in Virginia. Just as the Virginia Dare marker matters to constructions of nation and heterosexuality in colonial America, my attention to the Occaneechi in this examination of Adam and Eve highlights the heterosexed territories implicit in U.S. founding documents that secure the practice of sexual freedom for some, while ensuring the historic and ongoing gender and sexual oppression of others. Just as the nineteenth-century marker highlights Christian rituals and practices, Adam and Eve's name and logo do the same.

We need now only contextualize this ongoing device within settler colonial logic.

Archaeologists from the University of North Carolina uncovered evidence of the Occaneechi village and forts in 1983, but Dawes Commission rolls cannot duly document all members of the tribe since there was little interest by the federal government in "giving" tribal recognition. The evidence of the Occaneechi's existence has a different outcome than that of Virginia Dare. Scholars of Indigenous studies and Black studies argue that even if people of color are heterosexual, they and their families remain unequal under the cover of marriage. For example, historian Tiya Miles details the settler logics devised around Black and Native identity and intimacies to make marital and paternal claims to land invalid, explaining that "the 'one-drop rule' ensured that there would be more black laborers for slavery's human machine, while the blood quantum ratio ensured that there would be more available land for white settlement and development."[9] As a result of visual markers of blackness, or interracial sexual relations, many of the descendants of the tribe were later read or designated as mixed-race or "colored" (Indian/white, Indian/African, and any multiracial combinations) throughout the nineteenth and twentieth centuries. In addition to disqualifying multiracial children from tribal recognition, Virginia "first banned interracial marriages" in the 1600s: in the 1700s, "North Carolina lawmakers levied 'an additional tax on ... Mulattoes, Mustees.'"[10]

Laws such as these are why modes of sexual resistance in land politics might be overlooked in the contemporary South. When the Occaneechi Homeland Preservation Project began in 2002 in Alamance County, its purpose was to reacquire their land and ensure its ownership for future generations of the tribe. Their vision, however, also signaled a rejection of the centuries-old impact of allotment ideologies. For example, as Lesley M. Gray-beal outlines in her discussion of the Occaneechi Homeland Pres-ervation Project, there was a conscious effort to reeducate people about the tribe's history and culture: "Because American Indian people in the South were often labeled as 'colored' by nonindige-nous neighbors and classified as 'black' on legal documents follow-ing the Indian Removal period, regardless of whether or not they had any African American ancestry, many of the present-day Occaneechi people grew up identifying as black."[11] Choosing to not ignore histories of race, sexuality, and colonial management of nonwhite bodies, the Occaneechi resist settler colonial logics or "common sense."[12] The decades-long battle to be recognized by state and federal government means that whatever their blood ratio, individuals live their lives and plan their families around these laws and surveillance. From the Occaneechi to the Lumbee tribes, it remains clear that some would find joy and pleasure in love and sex shaped by culture and beliefs said to be decimated by settler colonialism. As one Occaneechi respondent told Beal, "There are many bloods running through our veins. That's part of the education that's not in the books."[13] Sexual intercourse or inti-macy that would be criminalized in cohabitating relationships or marriage if made public goes undetected on paper. Such moments are a model of family planning shaped by fugitivity and marronage as opposed to sexual freedom and sexual citizenship articulated in modern sexual health industries and reproductive technologies. Without land or the sovereignty promised with recognition, the practice of sexual freedom remains compromised, but rearrange-ment of space away from colonial logics produces mobility and resistance—sexual futurity.

BACK TO THE FUTURE'S PAST

Though its origins were in family planning, Adam and Eve shifted away from a biopolitical focus on reproductive control, and toward a general rights discourse about freedom of expression. Despite Jesse Helms's sixteen years of showcasing conservative sexual politics in the state, PHE had escaped scrutiny until Sam Currin, a Helms protégé and former aide, spearheaded an investigation into the company.[14] Not unlike the use of blood ratios, the tactic of quantifying what might be obscene ended up solidifying heteronormative intimacy and Eurocentric aesthetics and notions of beauty, eroticism, and sensuality. After being charged with nine counts of obscenity dissemination, Philip Harvey's eight-year battle with the U.S. Department of Justice ended with a favorable outcome for Harvey and his customers. It was deemed a huge win for First Amendment purists. However, First Amendment victories do not imply that Adam and Eve had nuanced sexual resistance in the South so as to challenge narratives of moral authority. Harvey's book about the trial fails to fully consider the significance of geography and labor politics. For example, in Harvey's account of the raid, he provides affidavits from his employees who were working at the time. Shirley Sell, a customer service representative, explains: "At approximately 9:00 a.m., while I was on the telephone with a customer, four or five men came into my work area with some sort of badges .... An announcement was made over the public address system that all employees had to go to the warehouse. I asked the man who had me get off the phone if there had been a bomb threat, and he said no."[15] Harvey's book exposes the ways in which everyday laborers saw their labor in sexual commerce classified as dangerous. After the raid, Harvey recalls, "The following morning, nearly every one of our employees arrived for work. Not only were they there, they were angry. 'What right do they have to do that to us? No one was breaking the law. Haven't they heard of the First Amendment?'"[16] Harvey unveils the complexities of consciousness shaping southerners' experiences with industry, sexuality, sexual expression, and sexual representation that could be classified as obscene. Yet, he provides only a glimpse of the labor that occurs outside of the acting and directing of pornographic films, especially labor that is invisible or erased in debates about moral authority and exploitation until it is criminalized as obscenity.

What were Harvey's hiring processes and protocols that yielded workers uninterested in biblical condemnation and moral panics? Certainly, in a right-to-work state where labor union protections are far and few, the untold narrative about labor and sexuality in the South seems far more interesting and complicated than that surrounding First Amendment rights. Especially since his labor force could hail from areas surrounding a university town, Chapel Hill (liberal, educated, with many northern and West Coast transplants) and the trial was held in Alamance County, a community known for rural farm labor.[17]

After the trial, the company hired professional sex therapists to screen all its films to ensure that no BDSM, children or youth, or other problem genres would be in their catalog. The resulting strategy, to medicalize their products as a method of disease control and heterosexual family planning, as they did early on with marketing condoms, is less about sexual libertinism. For example, years after the trial, Adam and Eve's marketing materials explicitly centered coupled, heterosexual desire and sex so that even if videos of lesbian sex (rarely gay men) were sold, their inclusion could be understood as in the service of preserving heterosexual marriage, desire, play, and fantasy. Framing its corporate mission around heterosexuality, the institution of marriage, and free speech, the company's profits and growth are of service to an empire that precedes the 1980s sex wars. Because specific religions have written binary gender and sex as natural, the sex company's logo and name align themselves with those moral narratives. Such a marketing move could be read as ironic were it not for the erasure of what existed before the biblical fable and the southern sex company. Unlike sex industry companies in California or New York that shifted regional conversations about gender and sexuality, in its decades-long existence PHE has not had such an impact on North Carolina sexual politics. Perhaps this has everything to do with the company's investment in and recirculation of the heteroeconomy.

Adam and Eve subtly showcases how contemporary southern sexual commerce in the South evolves from a history of settler sexuality, and arranges its evolution and tactics as an ongoing project for future regimes of settler sexuality. It also showcases how the issues of free speech and moral authority are deployed in ways that benefit some more than others. Corporations and organizations whose mission or vision coincides with preserving heterosexuality have been successful at avoiding State Religious Freedom Restoration Acts (SRFRA) action, while propagating a culture in which sexual and gender minoritarians continue to be morally judged and oppressed based on bills meant to ensure the state's right to discriminate on the basis of religion and the power of moral authority. As the Occaneechi reveal, there are ways to change without relying upon a higher ground built by moral authority and superiority.

SOUTHERNERS ON NEW GROUND: LESBIAN
ACTIVIST IMAGINATION

Labor studies and histories comprehend the importance of the body and physical movement to land, but writers and artists have effectively comprehended the significance of imagination and psychic movement as important to thinking outside the boundaries of colonial land politics. The ability to reimagine the Old South's segregationist models of spatialization required individuals who could turn to these alternative ideologies about land and relationships to the land. To return to earlier discussions about lesbian resistance in the South, in almost every piece of *Sinister Wisdom's* special issue "Hot Spots," testimony from white women reveals how white some of the events and organizations were at the time and records their caveats that they could have done more to get women of color involved. Notably Laurel Ferejohn's "Our Own Place" provides a history about the southern organization One's Own Place, an organization founded by lesbian feminist activists from Raleigh, Durham, and Chapel Hill in 1985. Member Meryl Sloan relays: "We failed in some aspects—most crucially, our overwhelmingly white group did not at all reflect the makeup of Durham and the greater Triangle area."[18] Ferejohn documents an admission about the failures around racial coalitions, even in an area as diverse as Durham, North Carolina. Southerners on New Ground (SONG) cofounder Mandy Carter served on the board of One's Own Place. No other woman of color did.[19] The history of settler colonialism and segregation underscores why these failures happened, and in some sense how and why radical lesbian identity cannot be sustained in the New South without developing more radical coalitional politics around race and deconstructing biopolitical gender. Nevertheless, the failures of some lesbians to address the differences shaping same-sex love, desire, cultures, and communities would shape the radical coalition politics of one political group and lesbian magazine emerging in the 1990s Dirty South.

SONG was cofounded by a group of Black and white lesbians with antiracist and Black feminist politics who were born in or migrated to the South. Mandy Carter, Mab Segrest, Joanne Garner, Suzanne Pharr, and Pat Hussain were the early nucleus. When the National Gay and Lesbian Task Force lost a site for its Creating Change Conference, which had been scheduled to be held in New York in 1993, organizer Ivy Young contacted Carter to see if she could find a site. She found a space in Durham. Responding to northern criticism as to why the conference was being held where Jesse Helms had reigned for decades, Carter's response showcased that her approach on getting things done was head-on and confrontational: "We're holding it in North Carolina precisely because that's where Jesse Helms is from!" Carter, Pharr, Segrest, and Hussain developed a workshop panel on organizing and making a life in the South. Joan Gardner would join SONG after that first conference.[20] True to the mission stated on its website, SONG "work[s] to build and maintain a Southern LGBTQ infrastructure for organizers strong enough to combat the Southern-specific strategy of the Right to divide and conquer Southern oppressed communities using the tools of rural isolation, Right-wing Christian infrastructure, racism, environmental degradation, and economic oppression."[21] The group would later change from being a women-only-led organization but maintain its commitment to intersectional, antiracist feminist politics.

The women involved in the early formation of the group epitomize how refusing the power of segregationist politics shaped their approaches to emerging social issues. They also had very specific reasons for why they identified as lesbian, feminist, or lesbian-feminist. For example, Hussain explained, "Being a 'lesbian-feminist' always got in my way. I didn't want to belong to an organization that was predominantly white, because there's always that push. It's kind of like swimming through molasses. That there's so much unintentional harm done, that I didn't feel like doing that any more. I just didn't want to do it. I didn't want to be a 'lesbian.' Again, it becomes about race."[22] In her statement, Hussain, who identifies as homosexual, further complicates concerns about the loss of lesbian identity. She emphasizes how even before the arrival of gender nonconforming identities, some people disidentified with the "lesbian" term and identity for reasons related to race and culture.

SONG started with a mission of "building transformative models of organizing in the South" with coleadership and codirectors. According to Carter, "A key thing that was important for the six of us was how to take what we were working on and show that it wasn't just about us, it wasn't just about being a lesbian, or a Southerner—what would be the thing we could take anywhere in the South that would let us sit at a number of different tables, that were not gay? One of the first things we did was to pick a non-gay issue around economic justice."[23] As Carter noted in her interview with me, making intersectionality a part of the organization's mission was not initially an assumption that members outside of the executive board shared.[24] Nevertheless, SONG. has accomplished a great deal for LGBTQ people living in the South, including "crafting the first-ever Southern, LGBTQ-led, traveling Organizing School for small towns and rural places all over the South; training over 100 Southern and national racial and economic justice organizations to integrate work around homophobia and transphobia into their work; holding over 50 Southern sub-regional retreats for Southern Queer People of

Color .... Most recently, the coalition-strong campaign in GA where SONG was central in winning an injunction against a key aspect of HB 87, wherein 'harboring of illegal aliens' was made punishable by law for individuals and organizations."[25]

SONG's intersectional politics were not developed via judicial challenges alone. Many members provide commentary that highlights the role lesbian literature, criticism, poetry, and music played in the formation of their collaborative endeavors. Carter and two other women, Michelle Crone and Barbara Savage, were organizers of the Rhymefest music festival, which took place in the South over the course of seven years. Their attention to the role culture played in the organization is emphasized by other early members as well. When asked about the origins of the group's name, Hussain explains, "We were out walking in the woods and someone said 'southerners on new ground' because we were out walking, and Mab said 'SONG!' And that's how it was named."[26] Joan Garner's recollection of the naming, while slightly different, indicates a similar experience, "I said we needed a name connected with the South—culture, music, food—a name with a cultural ring to it. And we came up with SONG as an acronym, and then we made up the words to go with the acronym." Garner also explained the role of feminist theory in her own organizing with SONG: "I read a lot of Simone de Beauvoir (as well as Audre Lorde and Barbara Smith). Women (and men) who are independent thinkers, and who call themselves 'feminist.'"[27]

The printing press and pen were not the only public spaces where the lesbian imagination was being cultivated and space reimagined. The few lesbian bars that existed in the South provided another space. Social geographer Liz Bondi, in her early studies of gender and urban spaces, explained that "feminist geographers have demonstrated a close connection between restructuring of urban space and changing definitions of gender identity and gender difference."[28] Gentrification and gay identity have been discussed a great deal, but much less discussion has happened around lesbian bars and clubs and feminist activist practices. In southern states, the opening and closing of lesbian bars are linked with two types of segregation: gender segregation and racial segregation. Bars must be economically supported by the communities in which they reside, but there must also be an understanding of the culture being maintained and created. Activists understand that shifts in cultural ideologies around gender and racial apartheid are important to building new institutions reflective of class, race, and gender coalitions. For example, when Jade River discussed opening her lesbian bar, Mother's Brew, in Louisville in the 1970s, she noted the difficulties she faced, despite having money: "My family owned several corporations in Louisville, and I had some business experience. I incorporated and sold stock to open a women's bar where we could be safe. We began looking for a space for the bar. People would not rent to us because we were opening a queer bar."[29] When they were able to finally find a space, it was linked with illicit economies: "I didn't realize we were renting from a bookie connected to the Mafia. There are bookies in Louisville because of the racetrack." She continues, "Because it had been a Mafia bar, it had a speakeasy door with a window. You could see outside without opening the door. The bar also had a secret door that opened onto a balcony in the alley. If there were someone at risk by being a lesbian (a local official, a teacher, or minister), we would show her the secret door. If police came, we would turn on the work lights. It was the signal to use the secret door."[30] The bar was both a leisure venue and an activist space. Operating at a time when discretion was necessary in southern cities edging towards being more progressive, in spite of aboveground conservative politics, Mother's Brew's belowground existence was not unlike that of bars in other southern cities. When SONG member Hussain recalls her early days in Atlanta, she explains the discretion of bar culture as pivotal to her coming out, saying, "So, I started going to a bar called Numbers on Cheshire Bridge Road ... quite sleazy little bar .... It was a lot of men, but there were also women .... There was a lot of dancing, and there were a fair amount of women, but mostly men. So, when I got there the first time I was excited."[31] Atlanta, as a metropolitan center in the South, became the center of many lesbian bars, including the longest existing bar—My Sister's Room.

Other women, such as Jaye Vaughn, recall such spaces as vital to the formation of their political organizing and activism: "I had met a group called Umoja, Black gay and lesbian professionals who met underground, literally underneath a restaurant with a back-alley entrance to a little room. They would meet, play music, dance, and have a good time."[32] From sleazy to back alley, the dirty was the basis of southern lesbian social spaces for a wide range of women. According to River, Mother's Brew "had some unexpected regulars. A group of nuns came every Friday night when the bar opened .... Hookers also came in, because they were safe from being hassled by their pimps." Rivers's bar subsequently became the meeting space for the Lesbian Feminist Union.[33] For all the sociopolitical benefits of the lesbian bar space, there also remained fundamental conflicts around race, class, and gender.

I want to return to the demise of lesbian identity in the face of new sexual and gender identities and the link of such a demise to the continuing impact of settler colonialism's land politics. Unlike what Gayle Rubin outlines in her assessment of LGBTQ clubs, I argue that the disappearance of lesbian bars cannot be disentangled from race, capital, and dispossession in the dystopic South.[34] Certainly, greedy real estate developers and urban development, as well as the lack of access to space and capital for women, are reasons for the disappearance, but these conditions were always present for poor white women and women of color. What has changed, especially in the South, is a fundamentally different relationship to the state and its policies around land, trespassing, and ownership. Even as earlier bar owners may have been racist, their cooperation and collusion with state agencies were curtailed by their critical engagement with state actors. This is in contrast to today's assimilation and use of the state to police racialized and non-cis bodies in these spaces. For example, in one interview of Mary Sims relating to her days with the Miami-based Lesbian Task Force of the National Organization of Women, Sims disclosed how activism took place in bar spaces, before recalling racism by one bar owner, "Lu, yeah she had a thing against black women. I think she refused to serve somebody. It was blatant.... the Lesbian culture was with the southern culture ... there was prejudice against color. We hadn't outgrown that as women."[35]

Another significant piece in the "Hot Spots" issue, Bonnie Jean Gabel's "Conjuring: New Orleans Dyke Bar Project," looks at artists, archivists, and community members creating performance art centered on the birth and death of lesbian dyke bars in New Orleans. The essay demonstrates why land politics are important to intergenerational conflicts about what it means to be lesbian-identified in the twenty-first century. One young person involved in the project outlined why she participated, stating, "I did not know what it was like to stand for days across the street looking in through tinted glass, dreaming about all of the dancing, kissing and organizing going on behind closed doors. I did not know what I was missing, but that does not mean I did not miss it." Another summarizes, "We wanted to know where it went, why as baby dykes and young queers we did not have that space."[36] These young people's inquiries exemplify why calls for lesbian spaces are not and should not be read as nostalgic, but instead should be read as advocating for a continuation of evolving lesbian imaginations for a new generation, some of whom may be gender-fluid. As Desmoines noted, lesbian imagination can be the most important gift a woman can bestow upon another.

Lesbian imagination that is intersectional arranges coalitional politics around cultural spaces such as publishing venues and bars, as well as deconstructs temporality and spatiality from racial codes. As bars have shut their doors, lesbians have continued to reimagine the ways land can be used to sustain marginalized communities. This includes configurations of space less associated with youth culture and bar/club nightlife. State refusal to imagine the lifelong ramifications of homophobic and transphobic policies, as well as the lived experiences of elderly gender and sexual minoritarians, require attention to intergenerational coalitions and allyship alongside hetero- and homonormative family structures. Once upon a time and far away from the South, ten architecture firms had an idea to build a gay geriatric living facility mecca in Palm Springs, California, called BOOM. Projected costs of BOOM stood at $250 million. The building was slated to begin in 2012 and end in 2014.[37] As of now it has not happened. Years later and far away from Palm Springs, lesbian developers Margaret Roesch and Pat McAulay developed their own idea for a retirement community comprised of LGBTQ seniors and straight allies in Durham, NC. They purchased fifteen acres of land and cofounded Village Hearth Co-housing Community, a proposed twenty-eight-unit cottage community. They broke ground on October 2018.[38] With goals of keeping things affordable and sustainable for active-living adults over fifty-five, the project signaled a concern for class, as well as sexuality, that seemed absent from BOOM's publicity materials.[39] As this venture is just starting, it will take time to see if differences of race and ethnicity will be taken as seriously as class in developing the community. Traveling across time and space in the South, efforts at sexual resistance and confrontations with the burden of sexual morality occur in queer labor practices and transactional sex outside of marriage.

SEXUALITY THAT TRAVELS

Despite the ways in which gentrification has been discussed over the last two decades, it is not merely a racialized economic issue in urban development. As ordinances regulating sexual commerce businesses and criminalization of prostitution demonstrate, the profitability of urban development depends and hinges on sexual moral panics related to the preservation of white nuclear families. Property values fluctuate based on the viability of normative social structures and relationships. While this concern used to be about the preservation of heteronormative nuclear families, LGBTQ assimilation into mainstream America has introduced the interests of homonormative nuclear family structures. Sexual moral panics as they intersect with concerns of wealth appreciation are a legacy of settler colonialism. Urban policy and urban politics that refuse to engage the dilemma of moral panics around gender and sexuality ensure further dystopic class stratifications.

When Texas Governor Greg Abbott was reported as claiming that Houston has more brothels than branches of Starbucks, he did so to advocate that more support be generated for the nonprofit Children at Risk, an organization that combats human trafficking.[40] Yet his words demonstrate why decriminalization of sex work matters in the Dirty South. As a result of new immigration and migration patterns, as well as changing economic opportunities and labor practices, educating the public about the difference between human trafficking and sex work and about the benefits of the decriminalization of sex work are major focal points of sexual resistance in the Dirty South.

Decolonial praxis requires us to bring a transnational perspective to these national ideologies. According to the work done by brilliant scholars of Caribbean sexuality studies, global and transnational sexualities studies change how or where an examination of labor and sexual resistance in the South can begin: "Can we speak about embodied sexual practices, identities, knowledge, and strategies of resistance of the colonized and postcolonial subject without lapsing into notions of essential native sexuality? Is it possible to explore the knowledge that is produced through [Caribbean] sexual praxis and to ask whether sexual resistance offers a potential for a politics of decolonization or narratives of liberation?"[41] An admission that sexual resistance in the U.S. South exceeds Confederate and Union histories, as a result of the Atlantic slave trade history and contemporary labor economies and immigration issues, means that we should consider the issues of space and sexual labor differently. Scholars of transnational and global sexuality and neocolonialism have led the way in thinking about the impact of imperialism and colonization on sovereignty, rights discourse, and economic policies related to gender and sexuality. Sexual commerce and sex work highlight the larger role shifting moral authority plays in land politics, but only when we are attentive to local politics around space and criminalization of particular sex acts. As Kamala Kempadoo's work has outlined elsewhere, sex acts are not simply anatomical practices; they are also economic and transactional. All are encoded with narratives authorizing their use or contextualizing their misuse in nationalist endeavors.

Carol Vance has assessed that "it is important, but difficult or impossible for some advocates to separate analyses of trafficking into forced prostitution from analyses of prostitution itself."[42] Vance critiques how such narratives enable other factors that contribute to trafficking to go uncritiqued, including "harsh immigration exclusions on the part of wealthy countries; ever-larger numbers of people desiring to migrate and escape the limitations of home and to access wages and capital; and conditions of local poverty increasingly produced by global economic policy."[43] A transnational perspective of sexual commerce or global sexuality becomes most useful in learning how to differentiate between trafficking of women and children and the consensual act of exchanging sex and intimacy for money—sex work. Further, M. Jacqui Alexander reminds us that such conflation occurs in a "historically intransigent colonial relationship, in which a previously scripted colonial cartography of ownership and production, consumption and distribution all conform to a 'First World/Third World' division."[44] The conflation of human trafficking with prostitution refuses the greater implications of this. White colonizers manufacture a simultaneous moral crisis/dilemma around work, gender, and sexuality that negatively impacts and oppresses those outside the regime of colonial power.

Criminalization of sex work, then, is a spatialization issue produced by colonization. Colonialism and settler colonialism in the southern United States erase this fact. A Black/white binary manifested in Union and Confederate histories creates a local literacy about race but not a global literacy about gender and sexuality. When sex work is written solely as a labor issue the moral dilemma manufactured by colonialism goes unresolved and the conflation of sex work with human trafficking persists. Rather than resolve the moral crisis of exchanging sex for money, resistance entails rejecting the moral crisis manufactured by manifest destiny and other religious ideologies of chosen (superior) people.

Exploration of the regulation and criminalization of sexuality in the Dirty South leads to an evolution of space and spatialization, and it also announces the arrival of innovators who change what sexual futurity can be or look like. Louisiana and Texas are two states that provide exemplary cases of how multiliteracies around spatialization matter to thwarting sexual terror in state policies aimed at sex work and sexual consumption in the Dirty South. According to Alfred T. Tribble Jr., an FBI supervisor who oversees the human trafficking unit in Houston, "Houston is fertile ground for trafficking because of its proximity to the border, its sexually oriented businesses, its diversity and the demand for sexual services."[45] Most of these sexually oriented businesses must adhere to particular ordinances. Such ordinances can dictate that businesses be between two hundred and fifteen hundred feet away from churches, schools, parks, and residential areas. Mandated distances vary by state and the type of businesses. For example, when Toronto-based company KinkySDolls, whose niche market is life-like sex dolls, sought to bring their sex robot brothel brand to the United States, they selected a site in Houston. Houston's city council quickly moved to expand existing "adult arcade" (i.e., sexually oriented business) ordinances to regulate "anthropomorphic devices used for entertainment." The city council, along with building lease owners, tactically used permit issues to halt development of the project.[46] The sex robot brothel introduced new concerns about how to regulate and criminalize prostitution and sex work, and it raised ethical questions as to whether the illusion of anthropomorphic companionship could lead to a rise in violence against women who do not behave like docile dolls. Not unlike Adam and Eve, the owner of KinkySDolls quickly turned to antitrafficking concerns to write a different narrative about his sex company: "We're here to prevent human trafficking. We are actually considering to donate a portion of our business to help fight human trafficking and prostitution, which is an issue for many, many years."[47]

Because he knows how antitrafficking rhetoric has been used in other capitalist endeavors, the owner strategizes around using income from the brothel in outreach missions. At no point in this controversy is there the necessary nuanced thinking about labor and automation, decriminalization of sex work, nor is there input from sex workers, as was the case when the owner opened up his business in Toronto. The sex robot brothel highlights why there must be more literacy about digital space, artificial intelligence, land development, morality and ethics, and sexuality in the New South. Likewise, when Trump signed FOSTA/SESTA legislation as a purported antitrafficking measure, sex workers collectively organized to bring critical attention to issues being ignored by legislators.[48] FOSTA/SESTA makes online websites liable for what users do on their site. It provided a moral victory for those who saw online sites as being unregulated and allowing the trade of women and children. However, because sex workers utilized sites such as Craigslist, Reddit, Backpage, Escorts, and Sugardaddy as an alternative to street prostitution and transactional sex because they provide a measure of safety for workers and their clients, sex workers posed credible objections to this legislation.[49] Since sexual citizenship seldom grants freedom around sexual labor, neither First Amendment rights nor Bible verses provide a solution that would lead to the safety of individuals who do such labor, address the gendered economic inequities that precipitate why such labor is performed, or acknowledge the amassing inequities that a tech labor force both advances and complicates.

Sex work is about economic survival as well as class mobility. Class mobility hinges on earnings and possession. Rather than relying upon domesticity's homespace to practice transactional sex, sex workers understand the grounds on which gender and sexuality are constructed as always shifting. They rely upon the body's temporal space and spatialization. Sexual resistance to sexual terror and violence requires this mobility and a different relationship to the land, one less based on homespace and possession. Though the dominant perception may be that decriminalization of sex work has historically been done by workers on the West Coast and in the Northeast corridor, several organizations in the South have been active for decades in challenging the criminalization of men and women who do sex work, as well as insisting upon a critical discourse that refuses the conflation of human trafficking with sex work. Several women of color-led organizations demonstrate a different approach to sexual resistance through a concerted effort to decriminalize sex work throughout the South.

In New Orleans, Women with a Vision (WWAV) has refused rhetoric that conflates human trafficking with sex work, and thus has been front and center in combatting state actions stigmatizing and criminalizing persons doing sex work. New Orleans remains a southern city whose blatant refusal of moral authority can be traced to its various and multiple spiritual practices, which produce complex expressions of gender and sexuality. Often considered a primary example of a global city, New Orleans has a history of sexual resistance to sexual regulation that is often traced to the once semilegal regulation of brothels and sex work in the red-light district Storyville, or to LGBTQ culture in the French Quarter. Today, WWAV, led by Deon Haywood and originally founded in 1989 by a group of African American women to respond to the HIV/AIDS crisis in communities of color, leads the way. The group provides community education about HIV prevention and testing, and it also educates public health officials about how to better serve communities and develop effective programs. Over two decades, it has expanded its mission to include harm reduction/drug policy reform, reproductive justice outreach, gender-based violence prevention, and organizing around decriminalization of sex work. WWAV created the EMERGE program, which funnels individuals charged with prostitution misdemeanors into community rehabilitation, and, once they have completed sessions entailing counseling, skills training, harm reduction, arranged for their charges to be dismissed.

However, WWAV's most significant work, so far, has been social justice programming thematically linked to a sex act exalted in Millie Jackson's "Slow Tongue." For years, WWAV crafted the NO Justice project, in which members worked tirelessly with other organizations to overturn or repeal solicitation of a crime against nature (SCAN) laws. SCAN penalized persons for participating in nonheteronormative sex acts as written in Louisiana state statute 14:89A, which states "Solicitation by a human being of another with the intent to engage in any unnatural carnal copulation for compensation. Louisiana 14:89 A(1)

defines unnatural carnal copulation as anal or oral sex."[50] SCAN
not only criminalized individuals for solicitation, it also ensured
that the specificity of the act would determine whether their
charge would be classified as prostitution or in the realm of sexual terror. The particular narratives of sexual identity, both historically and currently, that denote oral sex acts or sodomy as
unnatural must be challenged, but that can only be done if the
cultural and political texts meant to dismantle such definitions
do not arise from the same canon that produced the laws in the
first place. Understanding this, members of WWAV refused the
moral considerations of what is natural or unnatural: they also
educated communities about the differences between SCAN
charges and solicitation of prostitution. They highlighted how
the pieces of legislation centered on sex for money conveyed
two very significantly different penalties: prostitution was a
misdemeanor, and SCAN a felony conviction. Essentially, anyone soliciting and receiving money for performing any variation
of oral sex on another consenting adult would be classified as a
sex offender, meaning a pedophile, trafficker, or rapist. Moreover, if convicted under SCAN, offenders would be registered as
sex offenders for years. Understanding that the law significantly
impacted sex workers and LGBTQ populations, WWAV successfully fought SCAN to protect those populations. Their work
meant that individuals would not be criminalized and stigma-
tized, and their future potential to work or live anywhere in the
United States would not be impacted.

WWAV's successful activist endeavors depend on their will-
ingness to be fearless in destigmatizing nonheteronormative sex
and sexual labor. Their strategies begin with the lives and experiences of the people they intend to help and with cultural narratives that can help them intersectionally approach sexuality, gen-

der, and class. This does not come without consequence. On May 25, 2012, Haywood received a call informing her that the organization's office was on fire. An investigation revealed that it was arson. Noting that the crime was not a survival crime of theft, Haywood told a reporter, "There was tons of stuff in packages they could've put in the contractor garbage bags we keep in the office…. Twenty-inch monitors on our computers, all still there…. Either you don't like what I'm doing—and it's hard not to take it personal—or you just really hate women that much that you would do this."[51] Five years after the fire, fundraising campaigns and collaborative planning with Tulane's School of Architecture made it possible for WWAV's new space, Vision House, to open in January 2017.

Sexuality on the move challenges genealogy, public uses of space, and local land politics. It becomes clear why sexually marginalized persons (the poor, sex workers, and queers) become a threat to imperialist and capitalist arrangements of land. The Occaneechi, SONG, and WWAV have demonstrated why there must be a complete reconceptualization of public space and history as it relates to religion and spirituality, if gender and sexual outcasts are to survive and live outside the reach of hate and violence in the New South. In other words, we must understand what eating dirt means for us, for our bodies, and for the land, outside of what the cartographers of land and body tell us.

T.R.A.P. (The Ratchet Alliance for Prosperity) Manifesto

This is Lil La Laveau with the "Bitches Need 'Bortions Remix," featuring Midwife Mary. Shout out to the Afiya Center. Coming at you live from Dallas.... Midwife Mary from EUUUUTAAW, Bama and Lil La Laveau representin' Natchez, Mmssissippi. Spittin' rhymes for The Ratchet Alliance for Prosperity aka They Ratchet Abortion/Adoption Politics. T.R.A.P. Manifesto, y'all.

[Midwife Mary:]

Ratchet women are the witches and the bitches. Never trippin' over being called bitches and witches. True believers, the ratchet never trust in their god that much. We refuse a dream that we did not conjure for ourself: a nightmare, a spell malevolently cast. Men pretend not to know this. But witches do. Witches know.

[Lil La Laveau of Natchez:]

Bitches need 'bortions

Give dem babies back

And get your life

Since the courts like church
Only interested in a life
When it's miraculously written
In sacred texts as
Immaculate conception
White supremacist, nonviolent version
Or rigorously and scientifically explained
As a biological devotion
Loquaciously endorsed by hotepic conspiracies of genocidal
    notions

Bitches need 'bortions
Cause haters of Roe v Wade got
Historic aversion
To Georgia Douglas Johnson's "Motherhood"
And Casey an inversion of Gwendolyn Brooks's "The
    Mother"
Cause Rust v Sullivan bout diversion from L. Clifton's
"The Lost Baby Poem"
While Akron v Akron ... Stenberg v Carhart is a subversion
    of
Ai's "The Country Midwife" & "Abortion"
Bellotti v Baird a dispersion of
"Ballad of the Brown Girl"
Alice Walker's
Muthafuckin intersectional
Sentiments diluted into a singular
Legal potion

[Midwife Mary:]
Ratchet women are the witches

And the bitches
You must refuse a dream that you did not conjure for
    yourself
The nightmare … a spell … malevolently cast
Men pretend not to know this.
But witches do. Witches know

[Lil La Laveau of Natchez:]
Bitches need 'bortions
Cause bills
Be regulating and legislating pills
Pharmacists choosing not to deal
No matter what females feel

Bitches need 'bortions
Cause square-ass sexing
In the land of the free
Should not end with men
Manifesting our gonadal destiny

Bitches need 'bortions
Cause youthful indiscretions
And fucked up-ass Phils
Be talking bout don't kill
At the same time they steady takin
Straight-killin' a woman's will
Thinkin' dick way more 'portant
Than pussy
Ass-backwards politrickin'
Shit so unreal

Bitches need 'bortions
Cause rape, molestation, and abuse
On some misogynistic torsion

That should be erased not enforced
By personhood coercion
Oblivious to
Involuntary motherhood and its
Possible psychic erosion

[Midwife Mary:]
Ratchet women are the witches
And the bitches
You must refuse a dream that you did not
Conjure for yourself
The nightmare ... a
Spell ... malevolently cast.
Men pretend not to know this.
But witches do. Witches know

[Lil La Laveau of Natchez:]
Bitches need 'bortions
Since maya angelou dead
Her dusted-poetics not rising
Muthafuckin iambic
Phenomenally dosing
Lauryn Hill ... marching, marching ... late to Zion
But bitches' thighs not closing
Cause someone not she
Proposing and supposing
That she and 'nem
Shouldn't be steady composing
Without bankrolling
Without temperance controlling
Cause we all jonesing
And bitches' thighs not closing

We all jonesing

Bitches need 'bortions
Cause capitalism and democracy
Be stingy with portions
Have bitches begging, snorting,
Hooking, shooting, and extorting
Once the picketing, counseling,
And the waiting's over
Once the living exceeds the moral
Whimsy of charitable contributions

Bitches need 'bortions
Like momentum needs motion
Like dry and ashy niggers need
Lotion

Y'all know damn well
Bitches need 'bortions
To control, contain, maintain, and
Legislate they fortunes
To avoid being a state/statistical
Misfortune
Why this shit even still up for proposal

[Midwife Mary:]
You must refuse a dream that you did not
Conjure for yourself
Men pretend not to know this.
But witches do. Witches know

CHAPTER FOUR

Black women take care of their families by taking care
of themselves. Abortion is Self-Care.

The Afiya Center

Still D&C'd that shit, bitch.

Virginia, TNT's *Claws* ("Cracker Casserole"
episode)

Georgia happens to be uniquely positioned at the
nexus between the attack on abortion rights and the
economic impact of the entertainment industry. But
we have to understand that these bills are part of the
strategic efforts to overturn the rights of women for
the entire country.

Stacey Abrams

The dominant narrative about how women can lose or win
reproductive rights and freedom—so often compressed to one
facet, abortion—is one in which they must rely upon judicial systems, specifically the Supreme Court. However, in the decades
since Roe v Wade provided late-twentieth-century gains in
reproductive freedoms, cultural apparatuses have diminished
those gains in the twenty-first century. Culture remains important because it provides the forms, aesthetics, and narratives
shaping popular debates and legal arguments. When birth con-

trol and abortion were legalized, the most significant influences were quotidian narratives seen as depoliticized and private, in addition to scientific and medical concerns. As the twenty-first century has revealed, these latter narratives were always political and certainly cultural. They simply had been produced by a society that culturally valued science, empiricism, and rationality. Even as we exist in a society focused on technological innovation and supremacy as a way to maintain empire, such innovation has not precluded a devaluation and purposely misinformed usage of science and empiricism to uphold religious beliefs and doctrines that detrimentally impact women's lives.

The appointment of the current president of Planned Parenthood, Leana Wen, an emergency room doctor and former health commissioner for Baltimore, generated enormous hope for the future. Wen's background as an impoverished immigrant from a Los Angeles family who relied upon Medicare and Planned Parenthood, as well as her previous policy work in Baltimore, foundationally situated in social justice, made her an exciting appointment. Wen's personal and professional experience provide her with a perspective to better serve the vulnerable populations most in need of the organization. Progressives believe that she can fend off challenges coming from the current conservative state administrations and their perfecting of targeted regulation of abortion providers (TRAP) laws, as well as recent introductions of extreme abortion bans based on reductivist definitions of life and personhood that science or medicine have yet to unilaterally endorse. As I discuss later, I have named the latter CRAP bans, an acronym for "colonizing regimes over anyone's pregnancy" and "criminal rules of abortion prosecution." Responses from conservatives, moderates, and progressives have summarized Wen's appointment as a strategy to emphasize Planned Parenthood as a healthcare organization, thereby tactically depoliticizing controversial issues of gender and sexuality that arise from its radical socialist origins. Wen is a smart appointment, but whatever ground she gains for the organization and its rhetoric of healthcare advocacy will not matter for the Planned Parenthood centers and their clients in the southern United States. If Planned Parenthood is to survive in the southern United States, then those who believe in it must also insist on a cultural mission for the organization that exceeds healthcare, or generously support other organizations whose mission will exceed healthcare concerns. The basic premise of any family planning—individually, communally, or societally—is never really just a concern of health. An assurance that people who are not white or economically privileged will have some semblance of reproductive justice and reproductive freedom entails a change of culture around sexuality, as opposed to sexual health. The health of women, transgender people, and gender nonconforming people, as insurance companies, pharmaceutical research trials, laws, and government policies have historically shown, is not a priority for this country because their lives are not a priority. This fact is at the crux of controversies involving Planned Parenthood and the services it provides.

Southern states make up a segment of the country where there is little, compromised, or no sexual education. This region is a place where various forms of birth control, including Plan B and abortion, are still not widely accessible due in large part to religious objections. In addition, as in much of the United States, its poor are criminalized for their eating habits, sexuality, and attempts to access a better quality of life. Therefore, when any organization or popular culture platform centered on this geographical region chooses to address abortion or the abortion debate as about something more than medical care it means to change the culture and mind of the region. The struggles faced by such groups reflect how and why state policies create the continued conditions for gender, sexual, and class oppression, while also limiting options to overcome such oppression. Historically, reproductive justice and freedom movements by people of color in white supremacist patriarchal societies have radically imagined the abolition of forced, coerced, and involuntary motherhood away from Western and Eurocentric family planning models of empire and colonization by decentering white, adult, able-bodied, ciswomen. The tone and confrontational approaches of the real Afiya Center and the representational social world of *Claws* are long overdue, while the epigraphic words of political leader Stacey Abrams highlight the limitations of older modes of civil disobedience and the necessity of creating alternative tactics for gender and sexuality resistance in the New South.[1]

Although it is filmed in New Orleans, the TNT-produced television show *Claws* centers the lives on poor women of color and poor white women nail technicians in southwest Florida. In just its second season, the show unapologetically included a story line that demonstrated support for an individual's autonomy over her body and life, including abortion. After realizing she was not ready to have a child, Black-Vietnamese character Virginia decided to have an abortion despite threats of mob violence from clinic protestors before the procedure. By addressing all factors contributing to her decision, from the various stories of pregnancy scares and abortion offered by her women clientele to the potential father's perspective, the episode showcased the evolution of Black feminist cultures and the impact Black feminist voices can have on how the issue can and should be reflected. Written by Janine Sherman Barrois, a talented Black woman writer, the episode also demonstrated empathy for a television audience comprised of women, transgender, and gender non-conforming people facing a reproductive freedom crisis that won't be solved by means of conciliatory and compromising exchanges with people who do not care if they live or die. Clinic violence and the defunding of Planned Parenthood facilities showcase such sentiments. As Abrams's words allude to, the proposed Hollywood boycotts of Georgia film industry in response to abortion bans demonstrate that culture and representation can influence policy and local economies.

Afiya, an organization founded and led by Black women, often engages issues such as HIV and abortion in a manner similarly uninterested in government stereotypes or church beliefs about Black women's sexuality. Located in Dallas, the Afiya Center produced an advocacy billboard in response to a billboard from the male-dominated National Black Pro-life Coalition, which consistently demonizes women's decision to terminate a pregnancy. The National Black Pro-life Coalition billboard read "Abortion is not healthcare." One of this chapter's epigraphs is taken from the Afiya's billboard response to such misogynist messages aimed at Black women solidifies how a radical intersectional feminist praxis can be applied to an actual dilemma of reproductive freedom futurity. As the Afiya Center's website further explains, its "mission is to serve Black women and girls by transforming their relationship with their sexual and reproductive health through addressing the consequences of reproduction oppression."[2] They do so through political advocacy, cultural events, and fundraising. Notably, the Afiya Center's billboard was part of another larger organization plan led by SisterSong's initiation of the hashtag #TrustBlackWomen. As discussed later, SisterSong also works with the Southern Reproductive Justice

Network to address reproductive justice issues in the South in pioneering ways.

Afiya's deliberate choice to use the term "self-care," as opposed to the religious organization's use of "healthcare," is a bold move to redirect the conversation away from the medicalization rhetoric strategically used by pro-choice advocates and medical communities, as well as away from the morally authorized personhood language used by religious pro-lifers. As recent CDC data exposed, the maternal mortality rate of Black women is more than three times higher than that of white women in the United States.[3] The cultural billboard exchange, however, is part of a decades-long debate over efforts to detrimentally impact women in the South.

FROM TRAP TO CRAP

Five years after Democrat and bad-ass Wendy Davis filibustered the HB2 abortion bill introduced by Texas, and almost three years after the Supreme Court decided to overturn HB2, women in Texas and other states are still dealing with the remnants of detrimental legislature about reproductive capacity and control. According to various medical and public health associations, including the *Journal of the American Medical Association,* which examined the impact of the bill, more than half of the state's abortion-providing facilities were forced to close before the Supreme Court decision overturned the bill. Further, new clinics are still not being opened. Before May 2019, this legislation was noted as one of the most atrocious incursions on women's health and backed by questionable science, HB2 was picked up by other southern states that attempted to pass similar legislature containing the following fiats:

Ban on abortions after twenty weeks, unless medically necessary.

TRAP provisions: Doctors are required to have admitting privileges at a hospital within thirty miles from where the abortion was performed and that provides OB-GYN services. Doctors must provide patients with a telephone number of a physician or healthcare professional who can be reached twenty-four hours a day in case of post-op complications. Abortion facilities are required to meet minimum standards adopted for ambulatory surgical centers.

Ban on the dispensing of abortion-inducing drugs (mifepristone-misoprostol regimen) by anyone other than a physician.[4]

Notably, Mississippi, which has been the subject of numerous activism and advocacy campaigns and political documentaries, has one abortion clinic (Jackson Women's Health Organization) left in the state after years of TRAP provisions. In 2018, not to be outdone by Texas or by its own previous legislation (a ban on abortion after twenty weeks), lawmakers introduced and passed a ban on abortion after fifteen weeks. Mississippi also passed legislation enabling pharmacists to refuse to dispense Plan B to anyone who might attempt to buy it, after the FDA finally approved the drug for over-the-counter purchase.[5] What we witnessed in states such as Texas, Mississippi, Kentucky, South Carolina, Louisiana, Tennessee, Florida, and Arkansas, well before the appointment of a new conservative Supreme Court justice in October 2018, were necropolitical measures taken to TRAP poor women into a state of being: existing between life and death.

The changing definition of biological life has hastened the evolution of TRAP into CRAP bans. As of June 2019, congressmen in midwestern and southern states introduced six-week abortion bans to supersede previous TRAP legislation, and these bills have become the latest attacks on women's bodily autonomy. Louisiana, Georgia, Kentucky, Mississippi, and Alabama are the southern states using the concept of "fetal heartbeat" to designate personhood onto embryos in the fifth or sixth week versus the current legal prerequisite of twenty-four weeks, when a fetus is considered viable outside of the womb.[6] Despite the fact that some medical experts have insisted that it is erroneous to characterize an embryo as having a heartbeat, state representatives have continued to employ the phrase "fetal heartbeat" in legislation. Stacey Abrams and others have refused such language and have referred to such acts as forced-pregnancy bills.[7] Georgia can take credit for being the leader in such legislation, with HB481o, the Living Fairness and Equity Act: the act criminalizes anyone getting an abortion or providing an abortion, and it also includes language to suggest that anyone crossing state lines to receive abortion, as well as any accomplices to such action, may be prosecuted.[8] Alabama congressional members exceeded Georgia representatives by including extreme measures of imprisonment, up to ninety-nine years, for abortion providers, and by making no exceptions in the case of incest or rape unless the life of the mother is threatened.[9] These bans facilitate the trapping of marginalized persons into oppressive realities.

T.R.A.P.

Trap has taken on a multitude of meanings in this twenty-first century. Although it can still refer to a device commonly created to capture animals for food, clothing, or pest control, it has also become a term denoting a space where criminalized non-corporate pharmaceutical production and distribution happens, a genre within southern hip-hop culture, and the fascist abortion politics created by conservative citizens in the United States. I bring all three of these meanings together to discuss why a unique vision of reproductive justice and reproductive freedom has emerged as part of the New South. Doing so acknowledges what traps and trapping can offer to intersectionality. The T.R.A.P. manifesto highlights what some would call "them ratchet abortion politics," which I positively denote as The Ratchet's Alliance for Prosperity (T.R.A.P.).

T.R.A.P., as I am outlining it here, might be the answer to Cathy Cohen's question: "How do we use the relative degrees of ostracization of all sexual/cultural 'deviants' experience to build a basis for unity for broader coalition and movement work?"[10] Ratchet abortion politics necessarily complicate current visions of reproductive freedom reliant upon legislation because they do not begin from a position of human debt or the sexual immorality of women. Such prospects are extended to and advocated by and for Black women, as well as others. The Dirty South's psychic, embodied commitment to the land and the underground matters not only for heterosexual reproductive futurity, but also for queer and trans reproductive freedoms.

As a result of the current reproductive justice crisis arising from forced-pregnancy bills, political attacks on Planned Parenthood, TRAP maneuvers, clinic violence, criminalization of abortion providers, and pharmacists' invoking of religious freedom, it appears that the underground and illicit can serve as a mode of insurgency or militancy for reproductive freedom movements of cisgender, transgender, and queer people in the South, which brings us to the T.R.A.P. manifesto's revision of TRAP. For some, obscenity and militancy might sound an alarm about violence, but this is not the only element of these movements. Confrontation and covertness are also elements of militancy. The Afiya Center provides a militancy that has been missing from contemporary rhetoric in regards to reproductive freedom. Their billboard refuses to begin from a position of shame that sexual morality has created. Invoking "self-care" confronts the acknowledged lack of care states and religious institutions have shown in regards to the lives of women, especially poor women, transgender persons, and their communities. It allows mental health to become as relevant a factor in the debate as physical condition or the vital signs of the body. This is an aboveground approach that must continue, but covertness from the belowground movement must complement it. Here is where them ratchet abortion politics must be developed and supported. We are entering an era in which marginalized people will have to have a different relationship and engagement with underground and illicit economies in order for reproductive justice and freedom to be a reality for poor people, as well as middle-class and rich people. We will need to be smarter, safer, and more knowledgeable about our bodies, especially regarding the technologies, biotechnologies, economies, and labor forces impacting them. We will need to do so without the burden that intersectionality carries on its back: unacknowledged faith in the benevolence of the moral authority of the judiciary branch.

MORAL ARGUMENTS FOR CHOICE AND SEPARATION OF STATE AND CHURCH?

Most recently, biographical writing that centers people's choices and reproductive autonomy has been written by men and women who are either pro-life or pro-choice. One recent biography of a pro-choice advocate intentionally centers his rationalization for being pro-choice within the confines of morality-Dr. Willie Parker's *Life's Work: A Moral Argument for Choice.* Parker is also a board member of the southern program of the Religious Coalition for Reproductive Choice, an interfaith organization and movement that insists upon the necessity of making a moral argument for choice.[11] While Parker attempts to make this particular argument throughout much of the book, the closing chapter summarizes what he has articulated as a moral argument: "The God part is in your agency.... The part of you that's like God is the part that makes a choice. That says I *choose* to. Or I *choose* not to. That's what's sacred .... The procedure room in an abortion clinic is as sacred as any other space to me, because that's where I am privileged to honor your choice."[12] His book provides a smart and impassioned argument for women having autonomy over their bodies and family planning. The biography allows readers to learn about Parker's life and journey as a much needed ally and abortion provider. *Life's Work* should be taught in many gender and sexuality classes, as well as any pre-med classes where issues of ethics and gender are the subject, for the way in which it understands the arguments for and against abortion. However, in order for Parker's closing words to have the impact that he hopes they should have on an undecided audience, such readers would have had to come from a religion or a nation that valued women's lives and being. Unfortunately, that is not the case.

As appreciative as I am that a Black male doctor has been providing abortion services and advocating on behalf of women in the South, and that he remains a necessary and dedicated ally to women doctors and patients, I am compelled to deconstruct and challenge the strategy of insisting upon moral authority in his work, as I did for Reverend William Barber in chapter 1. This nation's inability to separate church and state when gender and sexuality are the subject of policy is why moral arguments for choice are a flawed strategy. Too much of Parker's approach is a mix between a spiritual conversion narrative and women's health advocacy. Rather than writing of a conversion from a heathen religion to that of Christianity, Parker writes of being converted from anti-choice to pro-choice. Certainly, the book is geared toward a less conservative Christian audience who may be unsure about or uninterested in the debates about abortion. Not unlike the Civil Rights leaders who organized the bus boycotts, whom he expresses admiration for throughout the book, Parker seems to be issuing a call akin to the one issued to would-be Freedom Riders in the 1960s. Instead of bus riders battling segregationists, he beckons to medical students, healthcare workers, and policy makers who have been staying out of the fray. He provides them with permission, a moral reason, to take up a righteous cause. Whether men and women will answer the call depends upon if they share the same faith as Parker.

In this scenario, persons who can get pregnant will be saved by those with greater moral fortitude. Because Parker's memoir must first establish his Christian belief and faith as an identity that initially opposes abortion, before converting to a medical authority and Christian humanism convinced of the health necessity of abortion, there is little to no consideration of how the concept of morality and moral authority creates the public crisis about a personal and private issue involving women's lives and bodies.[13] Thus, each time Parker makes a compelling case for choice that is based on medical and health concerns, as well as social conditions such as class, geography, and sexual violence, it is undermined by the limitations of what he is constructing: "a moral argument" foundationally invented and sustained by a religion whose creation myths represents some human beings as evil and already and always immoral.

The claim made to moralize choice is the same claim made to moralize the clinic violence and invasion of privacy that leads to doctors' and patients' lives being placed in danger. Parker discusses the death of Dr. George Tiller, the violence experienced by women doctors, and the threats against his own life as comparable to the experience Dr. King faced during the bus boycotts of the Civil Rights movement. However, a more useful comparison for this issue might be the history of abolitionists and Black fugitives during slavery, since we are not merely debating access and integration, but arguing about the definition of human life and who gets to define it. Such a mode of living is akin to the history of Black people enslaved in chattel slavery trying to determine and define freedom and what it means to be human in the eighteenth and nineteenth centuries. Parker's compelling memoir convincingly argues that the cultural narrative around the value of science and health for this political issue has shifted due to a conservative tide narrowly defining life and technological invention:

> Another so-called fact put forth by the antis is that "life begins at conception".... As a Christian and a scientist, I can authoritatively attest that life does not begin at conception .... So while the modern Roman Catholic hierarchy might regard each instance of fertilization as a sacred event, this belief is not—and has not been—universal among Christians. A thousand years ago, it was common for people to believe ... that fetuses only possessed what they called "a vegetable soul" up until forty to eighty days of gestation—at which point God imbued them with a human soul.[14]

Parker's language about the soul and this Christian interpretation of life have been ignored, but even this interpretation does not allow for separation of church and state, or other religious faiths that might have different understandings of soul, life, gender, and sexuality. However, Parker then offers a scientific discussion of life beyond conception: "An egg, unfertilized, is alive. And sperm are alive."[15] He continues discussing cells and gametes as alive—living organisms—and underscores that the biological definition of life provided by science has been overwritten by interpretations of a verse from the Bible, a book whose text and interpretation not everyone constructs their being and life around. This refusal to accept one morally authorized biological definition of life is minor in comparison to the ways in which the debate around life is essentially the refusal to accept women as moral, or more succinctly, the acceptance of women as already and always immoral unless they are made worthy and holy by a child.

Writing of pregnancy and obstetrics technology as a black box before "sonogram technology, which was first developed in the late 1950s and in wide use by early 2000s," Parker discusses how the antis construct a narrative around the technology of the sonogram in their reconceptualization of life.[16] Seeing the fetus serves as visual proof of life in the womb, or of fetuses as "babies—tiny people who can feel pain and are in need of society's protection," but as he notes in arguing life as process not conception, the picture is partial since the fetus cannot exist outside of the womb and "until twenty-nine weeks, a fetus can't feel anything like pain."[17] Moreover, this narrative of life insists upon an implicit judgment about potential innocence and known immorality. Thus, I would argue even further that the tide toward a pro-life, as opposed to anti-choice or anti-abortion, narrative shifted not simply because of the discourse of life, but also because of the ways in which patriarchal rhetoric has decentered women, transfolk, and gender nonconforming persons in the discussion of reproductive rights and freedom. Rights narratives too often seen as universal are already embedded with a prioritizing of men, so much so that reproductive rights, justice, and freedom are doomed to collapse back onto this priority. While men should be recognized as having some reproductive rights, ahistorical rhetoric that does not acknowledge that many laws of the land already recognize these rights simply refuses to acknowledge the inequality in power that places women's life in jeopardy. Parker argues that "antis seized the moral high ground nearly forty years ago, and they retain it to this day, because abortion rights activists, the people who have been fighting for the rights of women, have never mounted a significant religious or moral counterargument. Never mind that every great justice cause, from abolitionist to same-sex marriage, has been waged in religious terms, in order to influence or inspire the souls of the passive of the undecided."[18] Within this claim, Parker showcases his own male privilege. Women and LGBTQ people's rights have been successful only in the context of ensuring their like humanity to cismen. They, however, have never overcome the difference of sex and gender that is constructed out of a moral structure that places them as lesser than men. The antis can seize the moral high ground because they do not believe or do not care that women are morally penalized for their sex or gender. What is the significant moral or religious counterargument that women, transpeople, and gender nonconforming persons could make when dominant religions in the country represent them as less than men? To make a compelling moral or religious counterargument would mean turning to spiritual traditions deemed heathen, primitive, or evil. What is the religious or spiritual argument that would not have them branded as witches to be burned at the stake?

The reproductive justice movement does not arise because all human beings were being denied reproductive freedoms, it arises because marginalized people were being denied the freedom to control their reproductive capacities. Such a brief examination of the discourse of rights and choice and the discourse of life and personhood is not all-encompassing. It's simply meant to suggest that, though the two discourses are proposed as being in opposition to each other, they are linked through a controlling narrative: a shifting and vague concept called morality and its judgments about gender and sexuality.

Finally, understanding abortion as part of a larger issue about bodily autonomy and religion might be helpful. As Ashon T. Crawley explains, "The body is the tool of primacy in religio-cultural imaginaries and purportedly as a result, is constantly in need of control, of policing."[19] Both pro-choice and pro-life rhetoric direct ideas about bodily autonomy toward Western conceptions of body and spirit that insist on defining the body as part of a higher moral authority's grand design and of capitalist arrangements of society, as opposed to any individual's own design, which may or may not interrupt capitalist structures of society. People who can get pregnant should not have abortions and transpeople cannot transition because dominant interpretations of biblical lore suggest that a higher power orders life and living. Individuals become pregnant through God's divine grace, lesbian and gays get HIV/AIDS because it is God's punishment, and God made one's gender fixed. These bodies belong only to the higher moral authority that exists outside of one's self. Historically, as a result of either forced reproduction or sterilization, women and transgender cultural and health networks implicitly understood these damaging ideologies, and they deftly strategized around them to offer healing.

Many of the current controversies about health for women and LGBTQ people can be seen in the histories of how medical boards have primarily determined how women and transgender people's bodies are treated. Since that was not always the case, and because such dominance has not gone unchallenged by folks in the South, it is important to review how moral narratives are intrinsically cultural narratives that must be interrupted by different systems of knowledge. The history of midwifery in the South provides an example, and suggests that when community health models are coupled with illicit economies and futuristic technologies, the compulsion toward using moral authority to regulate women's bodies can be subverted.

RATCHET GYNOCARE

Though black women midwives in the South were sometimes known as "granny midwives," the term obscures how these midwives, young and old, were perceived to be ratchet by white male medical communities in the early twentieth century. Before TRAP laws and forced-birth bills, Mississippi ensured the mortality and disastrous reproductive health of poor and Black women through the legal system and through the American Medical Association, particularly with the 1921 Promotion of the Welfare and Hygiene of Maternity and Infancy Act or Sheppard–Towner Act. After the Children's Bureau of the U.S. Department of Labor provided a report that found that women were not receiving enough authorized medical care, the U.S. Congress passed the Sheppard–Towner Act, which was supposed to provide federal funding for trained maternity and child care. Good intentions aside, the act became a way to deauthorize the role of midwifery in the lives of poor communities. For example, twenty years after the act was passed, James Ferguson's study "Mississippi Midwives," explained that "In 1921–1922 a State Supervisor of Midwives organized the midwives for the first time on a state-wide plan in what was then a novel effort to lower maternal and infant death rates. The number of midwives actively engaged at the time was 4,209. Ninety per cent could not read nor write. Ninety-nine per cent were Negroes. The Negro midwives, being natural nurses, proved tractable, teachable and eager to learn 'the white folks' ways.' The less sophisticated rural midwife never acquired the reputation of abortionist as did her urban sister."[20] From the 1950s medical expert and writer, readers learn that earlier services provided by midwives included delivering babies, as well as providing healthcare with regards to family planning—including providing abortion via surgery or abortifacients (cotton root bark, pennyroyal, and silphium). Arguably, if Black midwives, rural or urban, were performing abortions, that information was not something that would be shared with any white male doctor or institution.

Ferguson also conflates race and illiteracy with lack of skill and professionalism. While textual literacy is a beneficial skill, it is not the sole form of literacy or the sole approach for teaching and learning childbirthing or pregnancy termination procedures. Ferguson designates both textual illiteracy and race as the reason for maternal and infant mortality rates. As Ferguson understands it, the natural mammification of Black women, when accompanied by white medicine, could possibly produce a more knowledgeable midwife who can then prevent a rise in death rates of infants and mothers. Of course, there is no mention of research done on what these Black midwives', or the Black mothers', lives may have been like outside of their labor. For example, did the mothers work throughout pregnancy, did they go back to work immediately after, were midwives able to return to them in time and on multiple occasions or did transportation needs impact the birth process? Ferguson further reveals how white supremacist ideologies shape the medical profession's dismissal of midwives: "In 1947, midwives attended to 23,815 (36%) of the women who bore children in Mississippi.... The training program, regulation, and licensing of these midwives by the State Board of Health have undoubtedly contributed to the 47 percent decline in the maternal death rate in the past ten years."[21] Such statements ignore other external factors that could have impacted these numbers: New Deal solutions such as the initiation of the Aid to Families with Dependent Children program in 1935, increased bus routes as a result of industry and city development, or access to medicine and equipment as a result of licensing. While midwifery still exists today, the dominance of the medical community and the regulation of midwives' duties continues to intervene on the autonomy of women's bodies. Perhaps this is why the 1960s and 1970s saw the advent of a women's health movement, even in the South.

One woman envisioned a similar path for herself. Byllye Yvonne Reddick Avery, founder in 1983 of the National Black Women's Health Project, now known as the Black Women's Health Imperative, began her healing work in Gainesville and continued it in Atlanta. Her early beginnings in Gainesville saw her refusing the trap of 1970s politics around women's bodies when she and coworker Judy Levy were asked by the chief in the division of child psychiatry of Children's Mental Health Unit, Paul Adams, to deliver a talk or workshop on reproductive health and reproductive rights in 1971.[22] Though she recalls not really knowing anything about them, she did the research and prepared a presentation with her coworker. After their presentations, she noted that women came up to them asking where to get abortions. At first Avery and her coworker did not know, but after doing some research they were able to make a referral. She explains, "I remember a white woman calling Judy and asking her about how she could get an abortion." They would refer her to an agency in New York. Later, Avery notes that after that incident more women called them: they would then refer them to the same agency in New York. However, they were forced to reconsider this strategy when faced with a dilemma of class: "A black woman called, and we tried to give her the phone number and she said she didn't need no telephone number in New York. She didn't know nobody in New York. She didn't have no way to get to New York, you know .... And the woman died from a self-induced abortion."[23]

Soon after, she and Levy found themselves in the feminist consciousness-raising groups of Gainesville reading *The Feminist Mystique* and *Our Bodies Ourselves*. She remembers, "And so, that was an incredible awakening for me. And we would spend months and months just reading for every single thing, every single book that came out—and sit around in Judy Levy's kitchen talking and dreaming. And it was there that we started dreaming about opening up an abortion clinic in Gainesville and we had to think back and be careful of how we did it, because we knew that the Alachua County Medical Society had refused Planned Parenthood when they tried to open up a clinic."[24] As has been stated throughout this text, literature and culture consistently provide women with a way to think and imagine around the systems of religion and medicine embedded with patriarchy and sexism. To dream of opening an abortion clinic underscores the lack of stigma and shame propagandistically used to silence women in the past and today. What she and others did was build and raise space and money via communities and anonymous donation, bypassing state agency funding. Once it was up and running in 1974, the center became something more: "At the Gainesville Women's Health Center we did a lot of education with women about their bodies, a lot of workshops and consciousness raising groups—a lot of things to help us understand who we are."[25] The center connected women with midwives and doctors. When Loretta Ross asked if the Gainesville Women's Health Center was serving Black women, Avery revealed her own preconceived notions about abortion and race, explaining, "And I really didn't think that many black women got abortions until we opened the clinic."[26] She expanded in a later interview, saying that "about 50% of clients who came in for abortions were Black, but not very many Black women used the well woman/GYN clinic. And that's why I wanted to find out more [about] Black women's health and what we were doing, and how our lives were being shaped."[27] Avery's experience documents how anti-abortion tactics can shut down basic conversations around autonomy and women's bodies.

Dreams and imagination also explain why the multifaceted labor of an organization such as SisterSong, out of Atlanta, accomplishes so much in its innovative approaches to resistance. Since 1997, SisterSong has combined grassroots mobilization with innovative media campaigns and arts and culture programs to curtail and fight against various policies intent on decreasing the reproductive freedoms of women of color. From the *Collective Visions* newsletter to the annual Let's Talk about Sex conference, started in 2007, SisterSong's approach differs from that of Planned Parenthood while also ensuring further support for the organization.

Led by Monica Simpson, SisterSong was responsible for creating the hashtag #TrustBlackWomen in 2018, as well as for partnering with other organizations such as Black Lives Matter. Simpson, an organizer of Charlotte, North Carolina's first pride parade, a licensed doula, a singer and spoken word poet, and a writer for various media outlets, has been a marvel across media platforms that reach a range of generations and audiences. The nonprofit SisterSong offers internships and leadership training programs for individuals and groups interested in bringing reproductive justice to communities.[28] They have been active agents in challenging the defunding of Planned Parenthood centers in the South, in responding to pro-life billboard campaigns containing genocide conspiracy theories aimed at Black communities, in critiquing North Carolina policies on shacking pregnant women, and in defeating Georgia's SB529, the OB/ GYN Criminalization and Racial Discrimination Act. A unique version of TRAP, SB529 was a racialized strategy calculated to reduce the number of abortion providers. The bill revolved around using women of color and ideas of coercion, with the intent of criminalizing abortion providers should anyone be able to prove that a woman had elected an abortion due to concerns around the race or sex of the fetus. SisterSong's efforts were to engage with and educate their communities, who could then act as their own advocates, and to counter the billboard campaigns meant to garner support for the bill.[29]

Other concerns regarding reproductive freedom and justice include adoptions by LGBTQ couples. Controversies related to LGBTQ adoptions demonstrate why medicalization of the associated reproductive issues is not always the best strategy. There are currently five states (Texas, Mississippi, Alabama, Virginia, South Carolina) that allow "faith-based" adoption agencies

(Catholic or other Christian denominations) to refuse adoptions to LGBTQ couples if they feel that doing so violates the religious or moral beliefs of the agency. In Mississippi, a state that does not have sexual orientation or gender identity listed in its antidiscrimination codes, legislators manufactured HB1523, which uses religious liberty to create legislation that allows discrimination. The bill legally creates explicitly heteronormative definitions that homophobic agents can use against LGBTQ applicants: "Marriage as defined as between man and a woman, heterosexual sex within marriage only, and that biological sex and therefore gender cannot be changed."[30] More recently, such legislation has been seriously discussed at the federal level: House Republicans introduced legislation to ensure that anti-LGBTQ adoption agencies can still be eligible for federal funding even if they deny or reject adoption applications from LGBTQ people based on religious grounds.[31]

Documentary filmmaking has become an effective cultural tool that feminist filmmakers have taken up to tell local stories of queer people. From Dawn Porter's *Trapped* and Maise Crow's *Jackson*, to Lara Embry and Carolyn Sherer's *Alabama Bound*, an activist filmmaking tradition has materialized with its gaze squarely on the South. Embry and Sherer created a documentary that provides an intimate glimpse into the lives of three couples impacted by laws in Mobile and Birmingham, Alabama. These stories aren't just about the legislation centered on same-sex marriage and adoption, they are also about cultural mores of the South that produce hate politics.

Although Yoruba Richen's *The New Black* focuses on Maryland's Black communities and churches, and their perspectives on marriage equality, Richen's promotion of her film has had ramifications for Black southern communities. Her film website promotes accessibility and outreach: "With your help, we can use the film to build bridges across communities and ensure civil rights for all in Historically Black Colleges and Universities (HBCUs), churches and other houses of worship, and cities and communities around the country."[32] The majority of HBCUs are located in southern states. As a result of this mandate, the film has screened in several cities in Georgia, Texas, Louisiana, Kentucky, North Carolina, South Carolina, Tennessee, and Florida. Likewise, in the recent documentary *Wilhelmina's War,* filmmaker June Cross highlights rural Black women's experiences with HIV/AIDS in South Carolina. Introducing viewers to Wilhelmina Dixon and her granddaughter Dayshaun, Cross demonstrates the falseness of scapegoating Black women for their lack of prevention and awareness. Moreover, the film's representation of grandmother, mother, and daughter becomes important to emphasizing one principle of reproductive justice movements: that reproductive policies must address conditions of life beyond fetuses in the womb. Throughout the film, Black women dealing with the HIV/AIDS epidemic go through enormous labor to raise awareness about the virus, raise consciousness about homophobia, and to obtain treatment, only to be thwarted by South Carolina's policies around Medicaid and Planned Parenthood funding, in addition to their own churches' moral qualms around gender and sexuality. The creative development of all these films is important for getting out information in an accessible format, but these films are also important given the ways in which the few progressive and sex-positive approaches to sexuality are too often overshadowed by dominant policies that silence information, facts, and awareness about a number of issues related to gender and sexuality.

Returning to the Afiya Center, the organization has combined concerns around reproductive rights with HIV/AIDS prevention and awareness to give nuance to ideas of reproductive freedom and justice. In addition to organizing the Reproductive Justice Summit and the #TXBlackWomenRiseUp hashtag, the center organizes the End with Red campaign, which combines their usual HIV programming with an "economic enrichment campaign aimed at developing micro-enterprising projects focused on creating wealth for women of color living with HIV/AIDS and those at risk."[33] The center recognizes that biomedical approaches to each of these issues will not be enough in already marginalized communities. In addition to these aboveground inroads, there must be a push for radical belowground movement, as medicalization and pharmaceuticals will inevitably come with conditions that must be navigated by economically disenfranchised and geographically isolated communities in the South.

FUGITIVE PLANNING AND THE RATCHET

As Lori Brown has documented in her book on architects and abortion clinics, *Contested Spaces: Abortion Clinics, Women's Shelters, and Hospitals,* there must be transformative collaborations and coalitions. Previously mentioned aboveground grassroots organizers have been planning for decades. Yamani Hernandez, executive director of the National Network of Abortion Funds, noted this in responses and protests to abortion bans, when she suggested that people support existing grassroots groups, stating, "We don't want to stop people from self-organizing. I think that that's powerful as well, but we just don't want people to recreate the wheel and we also just want to keep folks safe."[34]

Other coalitions have required a ratchet imagination, and these belowground networks have taken up fugitive planning and studying.[35] Around these issues of sexual and bodily autonomy, economic boycotts will not work in the ways that they have in the past with nonsexual political issues. In 1977, pop singer-turned-politician Anita Bryant's Save Our Children campaign successfully repealed an antidiscrimination ordinance that prohibited discrimination based on sexual orientation in Dade County, Florida. Because Bryant was a spokesperson for the Florida orange juice industry from 1977 to 1980, LGBTQ communities in Florida boycotted Florida's orange juice industry to attempt to make the state uphold the ordinance. They failed. In 1977, Florida legislators passed a law banning gay adoption, and despite the boycott it was not overturned.[36] Years later, the changing same persists. Anti-LGBT laws keep being introduced in the South, but economic boycotts of any industry will not be enough to cease the tide of hate masquerading as a moral compass and threatening women, transgender, queer, and gender-nonconforming persons.

Indeed, while there have been boycotts of states that pass homophobic and transphobic bills, economic boycotts over bills impacting the reproductive health and bodies of women (cis and trans) have been few. Is this because of the link between state agencies, corporations, and consumer cultures? Isn't this what proposed boycotts by Hollywood film studio of Georgia over forced-pregnancy bills indicate, or what Stacey Abrams's nuanced questioning of the economic impact of such boycotts on marginalized communities asks us to consider? Beyond these recent incidents, we might ask the following questions: How many states require gender reassignment surgery that might necessarily include sterilization in order for transpeople to be legally recognized via state licenses and documents? What role do health professionals in the cosmetic industry refuse to play in policies about hormone therapies and surgeries in healthcare? Does a boycott of any CVS, Rite Aid, or Walgreens over refusal to administer Plan B become impossible because of how medical boards, the FDA, insurance companies, and pharmaceutical companies control aspects of healthcare in nonmedical businesses? Does boycotting of health insurance companies for anti-trans discrimination policies seem impossible because health care is already gendered and gender identity is already medicalized? Does boycotting become ineffective because these companies' medical authority is being implicitly, and sometimes explicitly, determined by religious moral authority? Does it become impossible because pharmacies are seen as apolitical spaces, even as class and gender continue to shape how their local and corporate iterations deliver or don't deliver healthcare? Or is it simply that boycotting the pharmaceutical industry demonstrates the limitations of certain models of civil disobedience, and that these limitations indicate a system that cannot ever be equitable and so must be destroyed and replaced with something new?

Sexual resistance is different than sexual freedom, sexual liberation, or queer revolution because sexual resistance is rooted in a foundational knowledge that public acts will not be enough. Intersectionality as praxis operates in the publics and counterpublics, even as the experience of living through and beyond intersecting regimes of oppression occurs and proceeds from the underground and its imaginative movements. The public expression of freedom, liberation, or revolution cannot supersede the interior work and movement. Sexual resistance requires subterranean efforts because marginalized or sexually oppressed groups cannot access the public in the same way. As seen in the previous chapter, underground, covert subcultures once provided sexual and gender movements with protection or "closetedness," but there have been other uses of the underground or belowground. Assata Shakur once addressed this predicament as a flaw of the Black Panther Party, and the same might be said for my concern today. She stated, "One of the party's major weaknesses, I thought, was the failure to clearly differentiate between aboveground political struggle and underground, clandestine military struggle."[37] This becomes most apparent in the South where aboveground movements hinge on a history and nostalgia for a Civil Rights approach to every inequity simply because such an approach ensures an allegiance to patriarchal moral authority. Resistance in the South, on the other hand, has consistently been underground, subterranean, and unabashedly queer when it arises or lurks in the shadows.

Shakur's words here are important to how we can imagine sexual resistance in the face of dominant biopolitics in the New South. To be certain we should not confuse the underground with anyone's closet since, as Shakur notes, "an aboveground political organization can't wage guerilla war any more than an underground army can do aboveground political work."[38] The aboveground movements for racial justice and sexual freedom must continue to grow and evolve, but they must also be linked with an underground, clandestine struggle that can navigate the particularities of specific geographical and regional cultural beliefs. While aboveground protests continue, some of us must be charged with belowground covert actions. In what is now the dystopic South, the cultural aesthetic of the Dirty South has kept the old Confederacy from rising again, but it has not been able to produce a political currency that could abort long-held hatred and prejudice, preventing it from systemically and institutionally evolving into what it now has become.

In addition to advocating for federal funding for Planned Parenthood, we must all do better in contributing labor and financially supporting the aboveground work being done by the Southern Reproductive Coalition, SisterSong, the Afiya Center, Spark Reproductive Justice Now, Sister Love Inc., and free community clinics. Alongside this obvious strategy there is still more to consider. Here, I close by thinking about what the history of midwiving, along with T.R.A.P. logics, directs us toward: the incredulous and unimaginable. The things that cannot and should not be done in the interim—the efforts of a belowground movement. The criminalization of abortion providers now compels us to consider what writers Fred Moten and Stefano Harvey understand as "fugitive planning and black study," since grassroots organizations should not bear the sole responsibility of such effort.[39] Returning to Parker's *Life's Work*, I note it as a book that must be taught and used in order to question—and answer—whether the narrative of moral argument for choice, or lost concepts of civil disobedience for that matter, can truly compel a new generation of doctors to overcome fear of their criminalization to ensure safe abortions. Or will recent social justice activism in medical schools, such as White Coats for Black Lives and advocacy for abortion training, as well as humanitarian missions of organizations such as Doctors Without Borders to provide medical aid in conflict zones, need to apply similar strategies to the southern United States, as it remains a domestic conflict zone? Like law schools that incorporate critical race theory, medical schools will need to become radical places of fugitive planning and studying that finally understand the value of coalitions with midwives, doulas, and grassroots health centers as central to a network of safe and legal health and well-being options. Outside of these institutions illicit economies will remain important.

Forget cocaine, crack, molly, meth, codeine, and Xanax—there must be a wider network of hustlers, trap queens, and drug dealers who will cook up and deliver mifepristone and misoprostal (abortion pills, Plan-B/morning-after pills), PREP and Daraprim (for HIV/AIDS and transplant patients), and EpiPens, who will intervene on religious freedoms that impede autonomy, who will halt the pharmaceutical companies like Gilead from exploitative practices like raising prices on Complera and Stribild, since no one else in medical institutions will radically challenge the ways in which a national healthcare system and insurance companies refuse to truly contribute to the healing and well-being of all the people. This belowground movement makes aboveground approaches around civil disobedience more appealing, feasible, and expeditious to policy makers. Can illicit economies in which illegal drugs are produced, distributed, and trafficked become a model for what women, queers, transpeople, and poor people will need? Would that then be a real war on drugs? If any of this sounds too ridiculous for you, then remember, critical reader, that this is a manifesto. It manifests.

WeUsIOurU Future Pronouns Manifesto

Beyond y'all and 'nem, the existence of plural oppressions in the Dirty South necessitates the production of polyvocal and multiple manifestoes in this book. It acknowledges past subjects erased by arguments about Civil War monuments and Confederate flags, the Indigenous persons of the first nation and the arrivants displaced from other countries who have become fugitives in a place that never converted from white supremacy only from agricultural industry. These manifestoes are also for future subjects of the sexual dystopic South: the us (u southern? contingency). It is not for you of today who still can vote, for the we who still have First, Second, Thirteenth, and Fifteenth Amendment rights. It is not for the our who will not need to take up sex work to survive, or the I who will be customer. This is for the future subjects of the sexually dystopic South unprotected by the Tenth Amendment.

If there is a future pronoun of interdeterminacy and decolonization that will not require the grammars of a tense (past, present, future), gender, singular subject, or disassociation from a community, other than y'all and 'nem, it will be WeUsIOurU.

The time for being one thing or another is over. WeUsIOurU must simultaneously be writer, artist, musician, athlete, intellectual, comedian, engineer, and architect. However, this cannot happen via osmosis or magic (alone). WeUsIOurU must read and learn, think, and think about what is written and learned of the things we wish to become. WeUsIOurU, the writers of this manifesto in the sexual dystopia of the Dirty South, cannot and will not say who the WeUsIOurU of this manifesto is for since it could be for:

... future subjects of the sexual dystopia who have converted from a binary system of gender, a social arrangement of gender apartheid, and a spiritual belief in gender hierarchy.

... future subjects who no longer believe in gender, but who still like the feel and taste of differences in all the different types of pussies, dicks, asses, nipples, bussies, or agental-agenitalia that will keep changing the definition of what is sex and acts of sex.

... future subjects who will comprehend sexuality as a buffet of sensations that does not have to be cooked or served up the same way for anyone's gender.

... future subjects of the sexual dystopic South who will create a piece of art, write up a document, or create a code that will overwrite the birth certificate that regulates and legislates life.

When the future subjects of the southern sexual dystopias become who they will be by creating more original languages, narratives, and cultural art forms, that will give rise to new political systems and ideas. Once finished doing that, the future subjects will reflect and ask the following questions as a check-in:

Did WeUsIOurU make enough art and music for these new sex wars? Are there enough songs, sculptures, portraits, plays, dance performances, short stories, poems, novels, murals, games, posters, YouTube channels, podcasts, v ... blogs? Did WeUsIOurU make a synesthesia virus for when the machines take over? Does WeUsIOurU's binary coding color outside the binary ... RedGreenBlue? Did WeUsIOurU teach algorithms how to get down or break open a beat? Does WeUsIOurU's satellite differentiate between sex trafficking and international economic policies steeped in moral imperialism? Does WeUsIOurU's artificial intelligence know how to fuck outside of missionary position? Does WeUsIOurU's sharing economy understand transactional sex as part of its genealogy? Does WeUsIOurU care about consent, sexual violence, and coercion? Does WeUsIOurU differentiate between sex work and human trafficking?

If WeUsIOurU done figured out upon the end of reading this that some people are already this future subject and some are not yet, then WeUsIOurU must acknowledge the problem of temporality. WeUsIOurU must work against the current era's chronophobia and accept that the problem of temporality cannot be externally resolved or overcome. If future subjects admit or acknowledge living in this sexual dystopia, said future subjects must acknowledge WeUsIOurU's fugitive states and become the maroon doing all that fugitivity entails.

Be the red worm in the dirt.... Be the honeysuckle on the vine.

CHAPTER FIVE

Biological sex. —The physical condition of being
male or female, which is stated on a person's birth
certificate.

HB2, Public Facilities Privacy and Security Act,
Part I, Section 1.2

There's a target on every transgender woman's back
here. We have to watch our back, we have to be
careful where we go. You know, it's crazy that we have
to live in solitude, just to stay alive.

Paige Mahogany Parks, Jacksonville LGBTQ
advocate

Black pneuma, the capacity for the double-gesture of
inhalation and exhalation as the hint of life, life that is
exorbitant, capacious and, fundamentally, social
though it is also life that is contained and engulfed by
gratuitous violence.

Ashon T. Crawley, "Breathing Flesh and the Sound
of Black Pentecostalism"

Black (Trans) Lives Matter provides a conceptual
framework to understand the ongoing struggle in the
present by way of a future (aspiration) in which black
lives *will have mattered* to everyone.

C. Riley Snorton, *Black on Both Sides*

If they stop breathing … If they want to stop breathing … If their breathing is impeded … then no body lives. If there is more than a heartbeat … If there is Black pneuma, then there is life that will have mattered to everyone. There are no "moral movements" calling for ethereal definitions of sex or gender, but there are plenty of moral movements seeking to sustain definitions of sex or gender as biological, as that is the most actionable concept within the realm of state constitutions and laws underwritten by moral imperatives from monotheistic religious beliefs. Such was the case in 2013 in North Carolina and in Mississippi in 2016. How did the once-exemplary state of a progressive New South, post-Jesse Helms, find itself on the same page as Deep South Confederate and conservative Mississippi? Writer Jedediah Purdy accurately described the actions of Patrick McCrory, then-governor of North Carolina, the Republican Party, and the situation in North Carolina, stating, "In the sixties, as other parts of the white South dug in against desegregation, North Carolina's politicians found a different formula: accept the national consensus on civil rights and attract employers with low wages, weak unions, and business-friendly laws. The state's population more than doubled between 1960 and 2010, as a formerly rural, agricultural state developed national centers of technology and finance."[1] Purdy's article captured how the South's adapting and shifting economic industries coincide with social beliefs around integration. Moreover, the economic and social issues presented in his piece also account for what happened after HB2 was passed. McCrory and his fellow Republicans introduced what was one of the most anti-LGBT bills in the country since it sought to define gender in the strictest of terms, while making it difficult for cities to enforce antidiscrimination policies. Although protests and economic boycotts led to McCrory being voted out and HB2 being overturned (by the insufficient HB142), the tactic of using house bills to revise and rewrite who will live and whose life is of value continues. Seven southern states have considered passing "bathroom bills" like that of North Carolina. Four southern states have tried to pass bills that would hinder antidiscrimination policies, and five southern states have passed, or are attempting to pass, legislation that would limit transgender students' rights in schools.[2]

Beyond the Carolinas, there are many non-LGBTQ politicians in southern states who believe in the naturalness of gender and its certainty as a biological fact, so much so that they would risk a state's entire potential for industry and growth. Harming the state's most vulnerable populations was essentially the intent of the North Carolina bill in regards to other sections of the act. In addition to being anti-LGBTQ, HB2 was also antilabor and class-biased, since it attempted to curtail efforts to raise the minimum wage: "The provisions of this Article supersede and preempt any ordinance, regulation, resolution, or policy adopted or imposed by a unit of local government or other political subdivision of the State that regulates or imposes any requirement upon an employer pertaining to compensation of employees, such as the wage levels of employees, hours of labor, payment of earned wages, benefits, leave, or well-being of minors in the workforce."[3] Coincidentally, several of the southern states with anti-LGBTQ legislation are also right-to-work states that refuse to increase the minimum wage to fifteen dollars an hour, let alone enact legislation for a living wage. North Carolina's HB2 remains the perfect example of why twenty years ago Cathy Cohen warned that "only by recognizing the link between the ideological, social, political, and economic marginalization of punks, bulldaggers, and welfare queens can we begin to develop political analyses and political strategies effective in confronting the linked yet varied sites of power in this country."[4] As she outlined, politics and culture must be informed by a coalitional politics if there is to be equality. What North Carolina's HB2 and Mississippi's HB1523 demonstrate are states' capacity to dehumanize living beings through documents said to be for the protection and freedoms of a shared and universal notion of humanity. With each house bill passed or repealed, it becomes clear that many of these bills traffic in a necropolitics that adopts the biblical premise that "For the wages of sin is death …"[5]

This chapter examines the ways in which three African American performers devise their humanity through their own imaginative and creative movement, to counter a version of humanity bestowed by religious and moral acts and moral authorities. Each has used their music and sound as an articulation of sonic gender to counter the moral imperative of biological sex. In doing so, these artists also participate in class warfare and offer an example of a living wage that exceeds the monetary. A living wage is typically defined as earnings that allow individuals to meet basic needs. However, given that there is no universal definition of a living wage, comprehending the idea of a living wage as more than fiduciary becomes a key component to extending the definition of a living wage across all bodies: cis and trans, whatever race, gender, or sexual orientation. Here, the living wage also disentangles its subject from moral judgments. Before one can become a part of the governmental living wage discussion, there must be opportunity for employment. Barriers to employment and equal opportunity are key factors to understanding how racially marginalized, queer, and transgender folk can never do enough to access living wage jobs if they reside in states where everyday living is legislated as if everyone were straight and cis. Although there have been no moral movements to provide ethereal concepts of gender and sexuality, there have been movements to write gender and sex as something other than a biological natural phenomenon gifted to humans from a higher moral authority. Past, present, and future, this movement demonstrates the various waves of resistance to biological sex in the New South, as well as highlights a definition of life that exceeds biology and cautiously embraces a social meaning dictated by what Ashon T. Crawley, in *BlackPentecostal Breath*, understands as an aesthetic of possibilities.

During August 2018, bounce artist Big Freedia cameoed on Drake's "Nice for What" single. Though Freedia's signature voice was desired, she was not asked to be in the music video. The music video was released right before *POSE*, the FX series about New York City LGBTQ ballroom culture, finished its season finale. There are highs and lows to the publicness of being out and partially represented in culture; visibility as determined by its use value to mainstream expectations and social perspectives is not always safe or free. In Jacksonville the same year, three transwomen (Celine Walker, Antash'a English, and Cathalina Christina James) were murdered. The cases have gone unsolved by the sheriff's department; though the LGBTQ community worried about a possible serial killer, they had no trust that law enforcement cared about their dead or living.[6] However, to live in solitude, to stay alive, cannot be all. Cannot be enough. Was not enough for Celine, Antash'a, Cathalina, and many other transgender folk who lived in Black pneuma's double gesture of inhalation and exhalation. Cultural presentation of transgender life will not end transphobic violence or heal trauma from transphobic policies. However, it does create space for marginalized persons to counter the erasure of multiple systems of gender and sexuality derived from various cultures and spiritual traditions.

Breath. "Breathing," Crawley reminds us, "is not just a sign of life but is an irreducibly irruptive critique of the normative world."[7] Breath that makes possible Freedia's voice and bounce and made possible Celine Walker's love of dance and travel.[8] Despite the production of numerous bills to define sex and gender as solely biological, biological sex has been a category that many southern creatives could pose their way out of every day, as André Leon Talley has theorized. Talley, a longtime fashion icon from the South, has insisted that "it's a moral code to dress well."[9] Whose moral code, and will it be validated in the South? To dress well is about fashion, but philosophically fashion continues to be about exploring all the promises of any one body. Talley's precision with clothes and language means that the last word in his sentence is not colloquial. "Well," in his statement, refers not only to being stylish, but also to demonstrating one's spiritual, mental, and physical health. To dress well hinges on living life guided by an interior sense of self as opposed to being guided by externally imposed social meanings and forces. What does the spirit insist upon to be well? How can one fashion one's body to one's self? Breath provides the space to answer the question.

Years later, when an interviewer asked what song Talley would walk down the runway to, he replied, Diana Ross's "Love Hangover."[10] Runway walks are distinct performances cultivated by an individual's imagination and creativity and sustained by various breathing practices and techniques. Given Talley's southern background and the importance of Black church to him, the song fits perfectly with his insistence that to dress well is a moral code, a spiritual mandate based on the body as mutable. Anyone familiar with Ross's 1976 song release knows that there are two particular musical movements in the song where Black pneuma rhythmically and slowly aligns movement, dance, and style with the topic of resigning to illness or death, present in the opening lyrics, "Hah ... Hah ... If there's a cure for this ... I don't want it." From there, a shift into an up-tempo rhythm that sensually spirals and spins open listener, dancer, or runway model to express however the body feels from the inside out. Music and lyrics direct listeners to erotic love, romantic love, or self-love. Talley's acknowledgement of this song previews the theme taken up in the remainder of this chapter: how self-love becomes a love hangover that many LGBTQ individuals in the New South don't want or need to get over.

WAITING AND WATCHING: BEFORE AND AFTER BIOLOGICAL TRANSITION

Imagine, if you will, being somewhere in the segregated South of the 1950s. It's Sunday morning and a Black family is getting ready for Sunday school or main church services. A grandmother has the radio tuned to her favorite Sunday morning gospel show while laying out a meal of grits, fatback, and biscuits and molasses. Sunday is a day of praise and worship, as well as a day to reflect on how Black people will make it through the violent backlash being hurled at them for nonviolent protests aimed at ending segregation in the United States. The southern gospel quartet Little Axe and the Golden Echoes comes on the radio. The singular voice of Axe begins, slowly asking the acapella question, "Is there anybody waiting and watching for you," before the other three voices join in at the end of his question and repeat the refrain, "waiting and a-watching." Axe sings the question again as the refrain grows louder and the tempo increases until other imagery is sung into being. The song's dual meaning is at once about the Lord, or St. Peter, asking a question of an individual about to enter the gates of heaven, and also about communal responsibility, specifically watching out for each other. The voice is powerful, emotional, and unwavering, and while it gets answered with the response "my mother," the message about love, hope, family, and acceptance lingers for anyone who believes in the narrative about heaven and a life lived in accord with the gospel. Will they get to and through those gates, and will someone who lived their life right be there waiting and watching for them? In all meanings of the song, acceptance remains a key consideration. Acceptance, not tolerance.

Even without considering sound, the song's question and its preceding narrative produce a powerful query about how to live life. The song accepts a narrative about moral authority and its place in the lives of Black southern folk. However, the powerful instrument of Axe's tenor voice conveys layers of emotion ranging from quiet uncertainty and desperation to hope and joy when he sings that his mother, his beautiful mother will be waiting. Axe's voice also translates the emotional toil of the material conditions of the lives of Black people, whose survival depended upon community, culture, and perseverance. The looming presence of death could not be ignored, given the presence of lynch law, police brutality, and state policies detrimental to Black communities. To be right with one's maker was important, but the song also insists on a responsibility that we have to each other and ourselves to look out for each other.

Moreover, because of the lyrics and the vocal arrangements of the song, another unintended question may arise for some listeners if, like Axe, they are able to answer the question in the affirmative: Will those who are waiting and watching be disappointed by my nonarrival due to a life mired by "sin"? However, rather than privileging the narrative about Christian moral authority, I want to hone in on the second narrative, about community and responsibility to each other, about acceptance of one another. This must have been a concern that occupied the mind of Axe, who had been living his life as a transgender man. Born and raised in Houston with his older brother William, or Big Axe, who was also the baritone-voiced member of the Golden Echoes, Little Axe lived a remarkable life situated in what Crawley has noted as "an aesthetics of possibility."[11]

Halfway through "Waiting and Watching," Little Axe lets out a "wooo" that becomes indicative of breath's entanglement with the complication of flesh, and it is akin to what Crawley outlines as whooping: "Whooping, black pneuma, shows the capacity for the incarnation of blackness, as fleshy experience, to speak back to and against modes of violence and violation .... whooping says 'yes' to the radical fugitivity, to the lawlessness, of imagination, says 'yes' to the being otherwise than gendered, says 'yes' to being open to the world."[12] While much has been made of queer pianists and singers in the gospel music genre, much less has been said about transgender folk.[13] Hence, Little Axe's immersion into gospel quartets is significant from an aesthetic and political perspective. Based on Big Axe's knowledge and acceptance of his little brother's refusal of biological gender, this support by a blood relative signals how nonheteronormatively inclined family makes possible a nonmedical transition. Little Axe's years of performing in multiple gospel quartets, all of them male, become a transition rooted in the ethereal and spiritual. He does not have to be authorized by a psychiatrist or a priest, as his family and the gift of his voice gives him license to make himself. Little Axe was co-lead with singer Paul Foster, but his voice establishes the tone, modality, and breathing that genders or degenders the body and spirit. The remaining singers follow his lead and echo what has been provided. Within the quartet, Little Axe decides to avoid living in solitude just to stay alive. Each and every time that he sings within any of the groups he performed with, he embraces what the four-part harmonies teach about spirit and gender: acceptance. As a singer in the respected sphere of gospel music, Axe also creates a living wage: that means he is able to perform labor that provides dignity and monetary compensation on a consistent basis. As the secular music of blues and rock and roll increased in popularity, gospel music shifted from the quartet model. Neither of the Axes transitioned to secular music. Years later, Little Axe would die after his girlfriend stabbed him during an argument. While Little Axe stayed within the confines of Black church traditions, contemporary musicians in secular genres performing in the Dirty South provide examples more critical of Black Christianity and moral authority.

HOLY WATER

LGBT hip-hop has come a long way since its Afrocentric beginnings, traced to Oakland pioneers Deep Dickollective. West Coast and East Coast artists such as LeiF, Mykki Blanco, House of Ladosha, and Cakes Da Killa cultivated their audiences with unique sounds and personas befitting geographical and regional themes and styles. However, it wasn't until 2012, when Florida rapper Big Momma debuted his single "380," featuring Cakes Da Killa, that the South delivered another formidable Black queer hip-hop artist.[14] In addition to early singles, Big Momma has released an EP, *The Plague,* the album *Mommie Dearest* (2013), a Christmas track, "Black Christmas," and a recent single, "Jeffrey Dahmer" (2017), all to stellar reviews.[15] Noting his style as a mix between B.I.G. and Lil Kim, Big Momma, whose lyrics expound on his experiences as an openly gay male, exemplifies a Black queer resistance that critiques publics, elevates counterpublics, and most importantly, understands culture as sacred energy that can manufacture alternative ways of being human. It isn't just sexually explicit topics that make Big Momma such a standout, it's his flow on each track that indicates attention to the way breath can allow a gifted subject to slip in and out of body, of gender, and genre. This includes, in the tradition of LL Cool J's "I Need Love," creating quiet-storm rap songs such as "Penetrate," which samples a blues guitar riff before going into a smooth keyboard production and slow delivery of lyrics about fellatio and analingus.

Additionally, Big Momma provides Millie Jackson-style stylings on "Creepin'," where he raps from the perspectives of both a primary partner and the secret secondary partner. Big Momma raps about dark childhood issues on "Sodomy" and offers an ode to gender-bending on "Vagina Dentata," which deservedly got an impressive music video that mixed modernist and experimental imagery with BDSM, gothic, and religious occult symbolism. In the video, Big Momma dons red and blue contact lenses, a full beard and mustache, a wig, a full made-up face, piercings, and outstanding nails. With each endeavor, Big Momma works to undo the damage that moral authority has done to queer and gender nonconforming people. As Big Momma's website explains, "Unbeknownst to most, Big Momma uses his music as an outlet to express thoughts, experiences, rage, and fantasies that he could not, and to this day still cannot, express openly around or with his immediate family. Growing up in a highly religious Christian home and overall environment, he felt compelled to suppress a large part of his identity. This manifested in a fascination for the dark, twisted and explicit, as is displayed in his musical and blog content."[16] Unlike Little Axe's commitment to Christianity, Big

Momma's songs demonstrate a consciousness of how the South instilled a colonial genre of what it means to be hu(ma)n and what it means to be an Other, as described by philosopher Sylvia Wynter: "if *they* did it, how can *we,* the non-West, the always native Other to the true human of their Man, set out to transform, in our turn, a world in which we must all remain always somewhat Other to the 'true' human in their terms?"[17] Thus, rather than accept the assumed usefulness of common humanity in a moral movement, Big Momma engages a discussion that Cohen sees as missing from contemporary Black sexual politics. Certainly, his song "Holy Water" relies upon an understanding of Black communities' spiritual conversion in slavery and colonization to examine these issues.

As the song opens, before introducing his three collaborators, Big Momma warns listeners, "I ain't know it was gone get this nasty on them." Broken up into four different parts, the verses are split between one woman and three men. "Holy Water" lyrically details what happens when the blood of Christ, the son of god, and the savior of man, is replaced with the viscous sexual fluidity of human beings. Dai Burger concludes her rap verse with, "Who you know come through rocking a dress the fabric of a coochie sweater ... You need some blessings, I just pull up my dress and I make it drip drop like some salad on your dressing," providing a seamless transition for Anthony Foxxx to commence his verse, claiming "He on his knees like this nigga gone pray. Role play he do exactly what I say," before the third rapper, Will Sheridan, slides in with

Dick, dick, dick, dick
Gotta lotta dick ...
I'm a god, I'm a giant
You a giant's trick ...

I'm a father to the game
No religion
I'm about to convert a bitch[18]

All three parts include ideologies about moral hypocrisy, and they address subjects such as sex work, religious conversion, gender and sexual roles, and sexual pleasure.

When Big Momma closes out the song, he provides his refusal of cisgender heteronormative desire and biological sex: "I'm tip-toeing through the tulips. Booking trips just to get my pussy licked … make it wiggle while he slurping, lay my dick all on his chest." Big Momma authorizes a new genre of the human to exist, where redeemed spirit and fallen flesh can no longer be the basis of man. Since the blood of Christ is replaced with another body fluid, human desire made viscous (cum), gender is remade. Born from the pain and death of Christ is one form of the human. Big Momma intends another genre of the human, one made of pleasure and living that comes from self as opposed to an external savior figure. Sex, sex acts, sexuality are the sacred energies. His gender is based not in empiricist or empirical evidence of biological maleness, but in imagination and creativity. I build upon Big Momma's allegory in the line "Know/no religion, I'm about to convert a bitch" to think about social justice, economics, and sexuality for another southern performer, Big Freedia, Queen Diva from New Orleans.

BIG FREEDIA: PUNKS, BULLDAGGERS, AND WELFARE QUEENS GET DOWN ON THE FLOOR

The biologics of gender and sexuality in state policy continue to be threatened by the sonic constructions of gender, sexuality, and class known as trap music and bounce music. Bounce, the music and the dances it induces, continues to inform anyone in earshot about a different type of embodiment. It is both rhythmic cartography and class choreography that destabilizes the validity of biological sex. When all is said and done, in the same way gospel music influenced Sylvester, bounce music influences Big Freedia. Black pneuma serves as the dominant aesthetic practice that will show its significance to the artistic arm of a Black Trans Lives Matter movement, since bounce music depends upon holy breath. Given the dominance of beats and breath in bounce music and the affective benefits of the distinctive sound, my brief analysis of its importance comes in my discussion of its most publicly known figure, Big Freedia.

As Big Freedia once explained in an interview, "Bounce music is a happy music. And we use that to pull us out of ... all kinds of different types of situations. And when somebody puts on bounce music ... it definitely makes us happy on the inside."[19] Specifically, we should understand the ramifications of the music genre for those imprisoned by Western embodiment that arranges gender and sexuality into opposite and fixed binaries so that a living wage is impeded by heteronormativity. Beyonce's use of Messy Mya's and Big Freedia's voices on "Formation" as a call to arms relies upon Freedia's voice to equivocate a gender-fluid militancy that her own voice can emulate, as she follows up in a low register about her possible involvement in the Illuminati. However, Big Freedia's involvement in a southern underground movement before becoming a public icon of gender fluidity rivals Beyonce's agency as an Illuminati member.

On March 8, 2016, U.S. Attorney Kenneth Polite announced he would be filing federal charges against Big Freedia for fraud against HUD, claiming that Freedia had lied about her income to receive Section 8 housing vouchers that resulted in her receiving $34,000 to $35,000 in public monies. One story in *The State News* reported that Big Freedia "derived considerable income through ... entertainment and music businesses, including payments for performing concerts, starring in television programs, royalties, and the sale of merchandise .... [Big Freedia] failed to disclose this income to HANO [Housing Authority of New Orleans], as well as the existence of multiple bank accounts .... as a result of the false representations ... made to HANO, [Big Freedia] fraudulently received the benefit of Section 8 funds ... totaling approximately $34,849.00 between about January 2010 and November 2014."[20] Freedia's legal troubles exemplify why there needs to be more interrogation around how morality impacts discussions about public monies and public spaces. The linking of morality to economics, be it work ethic or sexual morality, creates a feminization of poverty, a dehumanization of poor people, and a sexual debt that not even fugitive publics or counterpublics can overcome, as seen with Big Freedia. Oppositionally, there also needs to be more work on the lack of remuneration for culture produced by local artists and icons that states benefit from.

Rather than doing as every news site has done, I want to refer to Big Freedia's own assessment of the situation, to write Big Freedia's actions as a figure who practices deviance as resistance, which is not legible in publics or counterpublics that continue to fail poor people because they maintain allegiance to Protestant work ethic and sexual morality. Big Freedia explains, "Housing vouchers are a vital lifeline for many people I know in New Orleans and around the country, including struggling artists. I truly believe there needs to be more programs for artists and musicians to teach basic financial literacy and planning. Coming from where I came from, I know that I could have used that kind of assistance. I'm exploring ways to be a part of the solution in this area and am looking forward to putting this matter behind me."[21] This statement says less about Freedia's financial illiteracy and more about her literacies in regards to what it means to be Black, queer, and human in the South. The fact that she is being prosecuted as Freddie Ross, and that every legal document referred to her as "he" though she has clearly emphasized her preference for "she," makes obvious that the state's criminalization of Big Freedia is certainly not about a concern that she has taken money away from the deserving poor, since in our current era there seems to be no such thing. Rather, it remains about how she found a way to access public money from a state institution that had been attempting to discipline her existence as a living, breathing, queer artist promoting joy and pleasure years before she became a public figure.

Big Freedia's previous state of poverty was determined by state policies that devalued the arts and humanities as not productive for the state, even in a place like New Orleans where Black music as cultural product has generated unacknowledged tourist revenue for the state, as a result of jazz, hip-hop, and bounce music's importance to the city's history and identity.[22] Big Freedia's state of poverty was also determined by state policies that would deem sexuality outside of marriage or reproduction, sexuality as joy, pleasure, and leisure as excess and therefore morally questionable and a reason to refuse her or her family any type of state help. In media coverage, there is little to no analysis of the early precarity of bounce music in the South, its near decade of underground existence and links with illicit economies of sexual tourism long before it became mainstream in 2000, or its importance to the rebirth of New Orleans culture. If there were, then perhaps any possible debts incurred in the underground in order to become a part of the public sphere, or amassed from welfare fraud, would not exceed the remuneration that the state would pay Big Freedia, Messy Mya, and others for its capitalization and commodification of bounce music. The criminalization, danger, and precarity of their cultural labor remains, given that moral judgments about the music and its movements (dance) can be prosecuted at the drop of a hat. In Hattiesburg, Mississippi, officials cancelled one of Big Freedia's events and threatened to cancel another due to moral panics and legislation that writes bounce and twerking as obscene and indecent.[23] Big Freedia's performances are seldom covered under freedom of expression but should be; most significantly, her experiences exemplify the importance of belowground and underground movements for destabilizing biological gender and the legal and moral frameworks that sustains it.

As Crawley has explained, we must all intervene on how "religion, fundamentally, defines the rubrics and meaning for ways to be human in place and time."[24] For Black people in the South, that means reimagining public spheres (health and education), as well as religion and spirituality, and challenging deeply vexed and entrenched erotophobia. We must imagine and reimagine a social justice and liberatory project around sexuality that is not simply about public health and private disease. Not simply about heteronormative or homonormative marriage or fixed sexual identities that allow politics to go along as usual. We must imagine new paths, remembering the undrafted cartographies, and shape a belowground struggle from there. Little Axe, Big Momma, and Big Freedia demonstrate sonic representations of gender and sexuality that record companies or public activists' platforms cannot translate into revolutionary energy or power. Can WeUsIOurU?

Honeysuckle, Not Honey
Sucka! Manifesto

The calls for a moral revival ...
                        .... moral arguments
                              .... and moral choices
                                    ...... in the South

Seem sweet
Like honey
In a cup of tea
More or less the same
Unchanging
Soothing in routine
And familiar
                        .... are for an Old South

What has been offered up for the New South, the Nuevo
     South, and the Dirty:
                                    .... a Slow tongue
                              .... Dirt
                  a Red Worm Deity ....
and a Honeysuckle God ......

By WeUsIOurU
Is neither immoral or amoral
Female, Queer, and Trans Insurgency
Is natural
Like all life-sustaining living things in nature
Must grow, sometimes wildly, above ground and below
    ground
Like vines that shade, hide, coddle, and embrace
Like roots that stretch out further below than the eye can
    see

Rise up honeysuckles, burrow deeper red worms
Threaten all that lie in your path
Nourish what has been displaced
Suffocate with floral and musk the cleanliness
Their perfume pretends to be
Shit all over what has been starved and emaciated
Choke it with your vines,
But offer your sweet dew to your peril
Men, moral or immoral, are not bees or hummingbirds

Be the red worm in the dirt. Be the honeysuckle on the vine

Honeysuckle … Not a Honey Sucka!

Coda

Despite public rhetoric that stridently insists upon the apolitical nature of teaching, teaching and learning have never been apolitical. Not for the colonizers and enslavers, and not for the colonized and enslaved. The dismantling of public liberatory education, be it defunding or privatization through chartering or diversity initiatives, intends to cease the process of decolonization that was initiated with the intervention of Black studies, ethnic studies, and women's studies in communities and learning institutions. Moreover, a divestment from arts, music, and performance in all centers of learning has also lessened the strides that might be made by those previously mentioned areas of study. Together, these factors encroach upon movements of sexual resistance in less visible and deadly ways.

Years ago, Gloria Anzaldúa explained that "We are taught that the body is an ignorant animal; intelligence dwells only in the head. But the body is smart. It does not discern between external stimuli and stimuli from the imagination. It reacts equally viscerally to events from the imagination as it does to real events."[1] What might our twenty-first century bodies need to remember? How significant is the imagination to resistance about gender, sexuality, and violence? In an undergraduate class on intimate partner violence, I have taught three short fictional pieces together—Zora Neale Hurston's "Sweat," Estela Portillo Trambley's "If It Weren't for the Honeysuckle," and Lynn Nottage's "POOF!"—alongside Critical Race Feminism law articles, and critical essays on intimate violence. I do so because these short pieces teach how, even in the face of violence, magic and imagination must be a first and last resort. Hurston's female protagonist in "Sweat" is saved from an abusive husband by a poisonous snake in a laundry basket. Nottage's female protagonist is delivered from her husband's abuse when she wishes him to hell and he spontaneously combusts. Trambley's female protagonist delivers herself and other women from an abusive man because she believes the honeysuckle gods cultivated and offered up to her the poisonous mushrooms that end his life.

In each story, women writers present nature as a magical and ethereal force that supersedes any religious institution's moral authority over their lives. For women of color, the fantasy of ending physical, mental, and sexual violence is both a militant and a magical process that is not captured by public protest, campaigns for votes, or reliance upon systems and structures whose foundation is male patriarchy sustained by white supremacist colonization. When the hope for something between political structure and anarchy or between morality and immorality paralyzes the less powerful, the magic makers find a way to convince them that radical action does not have to be violence by their own hand: that it can be the establishing of systemic confrontation with the fiction of moral authority. Their stories insist that the practice of magic can become a mode of fugitivity, a creative force to imagine the world away from the violence of men. Radical nonviolence is not passive. Radical nonviolence is knowledge, learning, and teaching magic. *A Dirty South Manifesto* began with thoughts on intersectionality, but it ends with a coda on bridges and tunnels.

As in the past, the work of Gloria Anzaldúa continues to be important in building bridges between multiple and diverse communities. When Anzaldúa insisted that "I am a wind-swayed bridge, a crossroads inhabited by whirlwinds," she was describing the burden that women of color are tasked with in saving themselves and others.[2] Her words certainly seem prophetic today as new whirlwinds threaten to break bridges that have already been built. Though Roe v Wade is still legal, the ramifications of "legal" and "moral" seldom apply to girls and women of color. Brett Kavanaugh's Senate confirmation proceedings for the vacant Supreme Court justice seat brought to the forefront of America the lives of three different women: Anita Hill, Christine Blasey Ford, and Jane Doe. Their stories demonstrate the ways in which the sexuality and bodily autonomy of women continue to be contained, controlled, disregarded, and misrepresented by white male patriarchy.

Before and during Senate confirmation hearings of Kavanaugh, it was revealed that an unaccompanied and undocumented seventeen-year-old immigrant girl, given the pseudonym Jane Doe, who had escaped abusive parents was denied access to abortion after she was told she was pregnant by doctors in the border internment camp. Kavanaugh issued the dissent that impeded her from having the abortion earlier in pregnancy, rather than later. Understanding the significance of this dissent, Jane Doe's attorney, Rochelle Garza, testified on behalf of Jane Doe and other immigrant women about the threat that Kavanaugh's appointment to the court poses to women's lives and bodily autonomy. She began with these words:

> There is no other way to describe the borderlands than a place where absolutely everything converges, and everything coexists. The reality is that our communities sit at the intersection of local, state, national and international policy, and as a result, our communities are complex. Our families are complex. It's perfectly normal to find a U.S. Border Patrol Agent with a non-citizen grandmother that he or she visits over the weekend in Matamoros, our sister-city in Mexico, or even siblings that aren't all U.S. citizens and fear being separated from each other should an immigration official happen to learn about their status.[3]

Garza provides insights about the borderlands that depict people still externally and internally struggling with settler colonialism. Her perspective exceeds the vision of African American former president Barack Obama, who in 2012 issued the executive branch memorandum DACA (Deferred Action for Childhood Arrivals), an immigration policy that provided temporary deferral of deportation for up to two years, renewable, for children who entered the United States before they were sixteen years old. As many less than optimistic and concerned citizens noted at the time, the application process could become a surveillance tracking system of children and adults that could prove harmful to them if a xenophobic president or House came into power. Such is the case now in the era of MAGA. The people who put children in cages do not believe in the snake god of Gloria Anzaldúa, or in Gloria Anzaldúa as a minor god. Otherwise we would not be here, trapped in a moment, debating and defending mostly brown children's right to live as fully in the world as we do in our dreams and imaginations. I want to believe in the covert existence of spies and infiltrators in ICE and the

Border Patrol, but there are too many journalists reporting stories about white, Black, and brown agents who rape and kill, and kill and rape women in the internment camps and away from them.[4]

Anti-immigration measures in the Southwest, when coupled with border militarization, produce human trafficking, sexual terrorism, and violence on immigrant women and children, in addition to exploitative labor practices along the borderlands and in the interior of the southeastern United States. For example, over the last few years, the state of Georgia has passed a number of bills that directly target immigrants. The Georgia Security and Immigration Compliance Act (SB529), which passed in 2006, states that employers must "verify the legal status of all new employees and ... provide documents on each person working for them" when requested by local and state governments.[5] Another example, Georgia's Illegal Immigration Reform and Enforcement Act (HB87), is an immigration act that requires employers to verify immigrant status and use citizenship as an employment eligibility factor, makes it possible for local police to randomly check the status of anyone they suspect of being unlawfully in the country, enables local police to enforce federal immigration laws, and makes it a crime to intentionally transport undocumented people or offer false affidavits about undocumented immigrants' status.[6] Alabama has passed similar laws.

In Georgia, these acts are complicated by a history that positions race in a Black/white binary, particularly in cities like Atlanta. In border states there has been a longer history of cultural exchanges between African Americans and Latinas/os: for example, Los Gorras Negras (the Black Berets) were a multiethnic group that fought for social transformation starting in 1969 in

New Mexico. Elsewhere in the South, however, dynamics of race are complicated with regards to industry and to historical politics. In their essay examining how Latino individuals are being racialized in the Southeast, Irene Browne and Mary Odem "argue that in moving beyond the Black/White binary, state laws that racialize Latinos create a two-dimensional category, with a homogenized 'Latino' category as one axis and an illegal/legal distinction as the second axis."[7]

In addition to these concerns regarding racial formation and immigration policies, there are also other factors to consider. In his speculative examination of labor and futurism in the Nuevo South, Curtis Marez attends to considerations of labor and technology when discussing agriculture robots and drones, particularly to the "struggle between agribusiness corporations and farm workers over technology—especially visual technologies such as cameras—as means for projecting competing futures."[8] Marez's study has implications for how the logics for and against immigrant labor have shifted and changed, while xenophobia and racism remain.

Calls for a moral revival or reliance upon moral authority also often overlook crucial populations such as LGBTQ youth. Currently, LGBTQ youth homelessness is at an all-time high. Churches and state agencies continue to ignore the problem for clear-cut reasons. As one national report noted, "the most prevalent reason for homelessness among LGBTQ youth was being forced out of home or running away from home because of their sexual orientation or gender identity/expression." More than half of the surveyed homeless youth (55.3 % of the LGBQ youth and 67.1 % of the transgender youth) reported this as the reason for their homelessness, and LGBTQ youth of color are disproportionately represented in these statistics.[9] Runaway and homeless

LGBTQ youth who engage in survival crimes are then at a greater risk for contact with the criminal justice system. When the True Colors Fund partnered with the National Law Center on Homelessness and Poverty to compile their *National Index on Youth Homelessness,* they ranked New Orleans eighth in the nation in efforts to prevent or end youth homelessness, and positively highlighted that Louisiana's decriminalization efforts focused on lessening runaways' contact with the juvenile justice system; but the report also suggested that the state needs to improve efforts centered on LGBTQ youth.[10] Fortunately, community organizations in New Orleans have offered an example of how to address racial and sexual justice around young people. Congress of Day Laborers and BreakOUT! created the From Vice to ICE campaign, which provides a decolonial approach to addressing the complications that arise from nonnormative gender and sexualities. In the booklet, organizers explain, "Vice to ICE is now the name we use for our campaign or areas of our work that recognizes the intersections between our struggles for liberation, as well as our intentional building with those whose lives are at the intersections of these identities—LGBTQ undocumented communities in New Orleans."[11]

Congress of Day Laborers was founded by immigrants and day laborers who were involved in the reconstruction of New Orleans after Hurricane Katrina. Led by men and women of color, the organization provides grassroots organizing addressing exploitative labor practices that pit communities of color against each other. BreakOUT! was incubated in 2010 by founding members Milan Nicole Sherry, Jonathan Willis, Lhundyn Palmer, Kenisha Harris, Amhari Alexander, and De-De Jackson, along with founding director Wes Ware, who later formally organized to create an organization committed to ending the criminalization of LGBTQ youth and their survival practices. In addition to working with Congress of Day Laborers, the organization has worked closely with Women with a Vision (see chapter 3). BreakOUT!'s We Deserve Better and From Vice to ICE campaigns have emphasized discriminatory policing practices in New Orleans as major political issue. The group's efforts are significant because they are led by and comprised of mostly Black transgender and gender-nonconforming youth. Their mission prioritizes individuals who are seldom considered in discussions of sexual rights and sexual citizenship, young people between the ages of thirteen and twenty-five.

Coauthored by BreakOUT! and Congress of Day Laborers, the From Vice to ICE Toolkit was created to address the Criminal Alien Removal Initiative, which was an Obama-era initiative that authorized raids of racially profiled communities. The toolkit also addresses the quota-based arrest practices of ICE and the New Orleans police and sheriff's departments. Interspersed with personal accounts of members' experiences with state violence, the booklet includes vital statistics and notable summary information: "Louisiana has the highest deportation rate per capita than anywhere else in the country, and New Orleans has the highest incarceration rate per capita than anywhere else in the world. Louisiana is also home to the highest per capita immigration arrest rate in non-border states and new data continues to show the disproportionate arrest of LGBTQ youth, specifically Black and Brown transgender and gender nonconforming youth."[12] The toolkit centers decolonial literacy practices that emphasize language and culture as relevant to activist praxis involving gender and sexuality, while also challenging the foundations of moral authority that might invalidate the prioritizing of gender and sexual marginalized communities and their sexual praxis. Understanding that its potential members may be monolingual or bilingual (English or Spanish), the tool kit begins with a statement about language justice, but it also includes instructions for carrying out nonverbal icebreakers to navigate the language barrier. From there, exercises to develop consciousness and community—such as story circles, a dance activity offered by a founder of *Two Spirit Journal* utilizing Whitney Houston songs, and a workshop curriculum—are introduced. Often assessed as secular practices elsewhere, dance and song are notable tools of spiritual and political intervention throughout the toolkit. The toolkit prompts individuals to engage their bodies and space differently than in political organizations where the secular and sacred are axiologically opposed. Notably, the toolkit does not critique religion or religious institutions. An appendix containing a glossary and brief histories of slavery, colonization, and gender and sexual discrimination (in English and Spanish) completes the toolkit. From Vice to ICE demonstrates the importance of transformational coalitions, multiple literacy practices, and a transnational lens.

Years ago, another southern writer offered a belowground perspective on the Black and brown coalitions she deemed necessary for what was coming based on immigration policies from the 1980s. It took Kentucky writer Gayl Jones decades, five other critical, creative, and poetic books, and words from her mother's creative writing to produce her last published novel, *Mosquito*. The novel is about protagonist Sojourner Nadine Jane Nzingha Johnson, aka Mosquito, a Black woman truck driver and conductor of a new underground movement, who "wants you to know the truth of the story, for the purposes of the revolution."[13] For Jones, transformative coalitional politics among Black and Latino people cannot only happen in the public, political aboveground space where prying white normative gazes look longingly, hoping for these groups' assimilation into the majority population.

As Mosquito travels the Southwest, becoming more deeply involved in the sanctuary movement of getting immigrants into the United States, a history and future beyond the current Black/white binary unfolds. When she talks to Father Ray, who is not an actual priest, about the sanctuary movement, she quips "But for a organization so secretive as y'alls, y'all got a lot of books about y'allself. Seem like if y'all such a secretive Sanctuary movement wouldn't be all them books on y'all." The dialogue continues, stressing the importance of underground work:

> He replies, " ... We ain't really the mainstream Sanctuary. The mainstream Sanctuary think that the more they're known the safer they are. That's why most sanctuaries declare themselves. We're more like the what they'd call the Nicodemuses of the movement. We don't declare ourselves."
>
> Say What? What's a Nicodemus?
>
> The ones who believe the more secret we are the safer we are.[14]

Throughout the novel, Jones makes sure to assert that transformational coalitional politics must begin in imaginations that situate histories, memories, and bodies in a place and time far away from those created by slavery and colonialism. The stream of consciousness novel drops nuggets of knowledge about Black and Latino histories and connections before and after conquest, as well as during colonization. As her Mexican and Black characters engage each other on their own terms, they learn more about each other. There is no successful insurrection without language, spirituality, and culture that have survived or have been decolonized. Once mutual comprehension is addressed, someone must risk being misunderstood for further truths to be unveiled.

The misunderstanding between these characters about the sanctuary movement(s) provides a fitting way to conclude this work's celebration of and thankfulness for sexual resistance in the South and its critique of moral authority in contemporary progressive southern politics. Jones's representation of the Nicodemuses of the movement as a nod to secrecy, or to secret societies within movements, suggests that the publicness of decolonization and resistance is not the only tactic. The pursuit of sexual and gender equity and freedom requires declaration and action, but it will also require a particular type of vulnerability. The Dirty South has proven as much. Thus, if we begin with the premise that decolonial sexuality and gender are as important to insurgency as weaponry and intelligence gathering, especially as it relates to what have been classified as asexual or nonsexual political issues, then maybe the foundation of insurgency becomes a type of vigilante justice that understands that law and legal measurements are already corrupt and cannot be the basis of change alone. Once the bridges have been built, we must have cultural architects who can transition those bridges into tunnels in opposition to the walls now being built. This is not simply about quests for citizenship and safety, but about new modes of being human and embodying freedom.

ACKNOWLEDGMENTS

I am thankful to have been raised in all the dirtiness of Durham, NC.

As always, I acknowledge my mother-father Vanessa Horton for unconditional love and numerous sacrifices that make possible my voice and life.

I am grateful for the existence and work of all the community organizations, centers, and entities whose efforts inspire chapters in this book: SONG, SisterSong, Women with a Vision, BREAKOUT!, Congress of Day Laborers, the Afiya Center, SPARK Reproductive Justice NOW, SisterLove Inc., the Sallie Bingham Center for Women's History and Culture at Duke University, the LGBTQ Center at North Carolina Central University, and *Sinister Wisdom.*

I am grateful to Mandy Carter for allowing me to interview her.

Portions of this manuscript were based on talks I did at Florida Atlantic University, University of Arizona, Arizona State, and University of California Riverside in 2016. People who engaged me and lovingly challenged my concerns about the South throughout those talks and during this process include Marlon Bailey, Darius Bost, Sika Dagbovie, E. Patrick Johnson, Kifu Faruq, Susan Stryker, and University of Maryland WMST 298 students.

I thank Lisa Duggan and Curtis Marez for allowing me to bring the South to their series.

To William and Mecca, thank you for loving me. Mecca, you have been a welcome surprise of love, laughter, and pleasure dedicated to exploring inner worlds.

William, thank you for being everything the universe told me you would be. Happy that I listened.

NOTES

INTRODUCTION

1. Deborah N. Cohn and Jon Smith, *Look Away! The U.S. South in New World Studies* (Durham, NC: Duke University Press, 2004), 1.

2. Cohn and Smith, *Look Away*, 90.

3. Zandria F. Robinson, *This Ain't Chicago: Race, Class, and Regional Identity in the Post-Soul South* (Durham: University of North Carolina Press, 2014), 1.

4. Janet Lyon, *Manifestoes: Provocations of the Modern* (Ithaca, NY: Cornell University Press, 1999), 10.

5. Lyon, *Manifestoes*, 8.

6. For contrasting ideologies in southern manifestos, see Pippa Holloway, "Manifesto of a Queer South Politics," *PMLA* 131 (2016): 182–86 and Strom Thurmond's "Southern Manifesto," 1956, reprinted in John Kyle Day's *The Southern Manifesto: Massive Resistance and the Fight to Preserve Segregation* (Jackson: University Press of Mississippi, 2014), 157–62.

7. Cathy J. Cohen, "Deviance as Resistance: A New Research Agenda for the Study of Black Politics," *Du Bois Review* 1, no. 1 (March 2004): 27–45, 30.

8. Deborah R. Vargas, "Ruminations on *Lo Sucio* as a Latino Queer Analytic," *American Quarterly* 66, no. 3 (September 2014): 715–26, 715.

CHAPTER ONE

1. Justin Miller, "Reverend William Barber Is on a Mission from God: Change the Country's Moral Narrative," *American Prospect*, August 22, 2016, http://prospect.org/article/reverend-william-barber-mission-god-change-country%E2%80%99s-moral-narrative.

2. Miller, "Reverend William Barber."

3. Frantz Fanon, *The Wretched of the Earth*, trans. Constance Farrington (New York: Grove Weidenfeld, 1963), 135.

4. "Smithfield Foods Introduces New Innovative Venture, Smithfield Bioscience," Press Release, April 12, 2017, https://www.smithfield foods.com/newsroom/press-releases-and-news/smithfield-foods-introduces-new-innovative-venture-smithfield-bioscience, accessed May 6, 2019.

5. Steven Greenhouse, "After 15 Years, North Carolina Plant Unionizes," *New York Times*, December 13, 2008, https://www.nytimes.com/2008/12/13/us/13smithfield.html.

6. Cathy J. Cohen, "Deviance as Resistance: A New Research Agenda for the Study of Black Politics," *Du Bois Review* 1, no. 1 (March 2004): 27–45, 30

7. Ben Westhoff, *Dirty South: OutKast, Lil Wayne, Soulja Boy, and the Southern Rappers Who Reinvented Hip Hop* (Chicago: Chicago Review Press, 2011), 29.

8. Carl Wiser, "Songwriter Interviews: Millie Jackson," *Songfacts*, May 11, 2010, www.songfacts.com/blog/interviews/millie-jackson, accessed May 6, 2019.

9. Jesse Serwer, "DJ Screw: From Cough Syrup to Full-Blown Fever," *The Guardian*, November 11, 2010, https://www.theguardian.com/music/2010/nov/11/dj-screw-drake-fever-ray.

10. See Robert Christgau, *Christgau's Record Guide: The '80s* (New York: Pantheon, 1990), 207.

11. See Robert B. Preston, "Millie Jackson's Revue Gets Way Down and Dirty," *Chicago Tribune*, October 15, 1993, www.chicagotribune.com/news/ct-xpm-1993-10-15-9310150107-story.html.

12. Barbara Hagerty, "Same Bible, Different Verdict on Gay Marriage," *NPR*, May 11, 2012, https://www.npr.org/2012/05/11/152466134/same-bible-different-verdict-on-gay-marriage.

13. "Why We Are Here Today," NAACP of North Carolina, April 29, 2013, http://carolinajustice.typepad.com/ncnaacp/2013/05/why-we-are-here-today.html, accessed May 6, 2019.

14. Sandra L. Barnes, *Live Long and Prosper: How Black Megachurches Address HIV/AIDS and Poverty in the Age of Prosperity Theology* (Bronx, NY: Fordham University Press, 2012), 177.

15. Eric McDaniel, *Politics in the Pews: The Political Mobilization of Black Churches* (Ann Arbor: University of Michigan Press, 2008), 158.

16. H.R. Report No. 104–664, at 21 (1996), https://www.congress.gov/congressional-report/104th-congress/house-report/664/1.

17. H.R. Report No. 104–664, at 41.

18. H.R. Report No. 104–664, at 48.

19. "Rev. Dr. William Barber, NC NAACP President, Speaks against Amendment One," College Park Baptist Church, April 17, 2012, video, 37:57, https://www.youtube.com/watch?v=bU45zdh9m-s, accessed May 6, 2019.

20. South Carolina General Assembly, 122nd session, "Marriage and Constitution Restoration Act," https://www.scstatehouse.gov/sess122_2017-2018/bills/4949.htm.

21. Alicia Cox, "Settler Colonialism," in *Oxford Bibliographies: Literary and Critical Theory,* last modified July 26, 2017, www.oxfordbibliographies.com/view/document/obo-9780190221911/obo-9780190221911-0029.xml.

22. Claudio Saunt, Barbara Krauthamer, Tiya Miles, Celia E. Naylor, and Circe Sturm, "Rethinking Race and Culture in the Early South," *Ethnohistory* 53, no. 2 (2006): 399–405, 402.

23. See "Our Moral Agenda," Repairers of the Breach (website), https://www.breachrepairers.org/moralagenda, accessed June 5, 2019.

24. Cathy J. Cohen, "Punks, Bulldaggers, and Welfare Queens: The Radical Potential of Queer Politics?" *GLQ: A Journal of Lesbian and Gay Studies* 3, no. 4 (January 1997): 437–65, 438; emphasis in original.

CHAPTER TWO

1. Alexander Woywodt and Akos Kiss, "Geophagia: The History of Earth-Eating," *Journal of the Royal Society of Medicine* 95, no. 3 (2002): 143–46.

2. See Minnie Bruce Pratt, *The Dirt She Ate: New and Selected Poems* (Pittsburgh, PA: University of Pittsburgh Press, 2003) and Minnie Bruce Pratt, "Eating Clay," in *Walking Back Up Depot Street: Poems* (Pittsburgh, PA: University of Pittsburgh Press, 1999), 91–93.

3. William E. Schmidt, "Southern Practice of Eating Dirt," *New York Times,*February 13, 1984, www.nytimes.com/1984/02/13/us/southern-practice-of-eating-dirt-shows-signs-of-waning.html.

4. James Forman, "Black Manifesto," in *Reparations for Slavery: A Reader,* eds. Ronald P. Salzberger and Mary C. Turck, 70–75 (Lanham, MD: Rowman and Littlefield Publishers, 2004), 72.

5. Jaime Harker, *The Lesbian South: Southern Feminists, the Women in Print Movement, and the Queer Literary Canon* (Chapel Hill: University of North Carolina Press, 2018), 7.

6. Harriet Desmoines, "Notes for a Magazine I," *Sinister Wisdom* 1, no. 1 (1976): 3.

7. Desmoines, "Notes for a Magazine I," 4.

8. Harriet Desmoines, "Notes for a Magazine II," *Sinister Wisdom* 1, no. 1 (1976): 30.

9. "Notes for a Special Issue: Hot Spots: Creating Lesbian Space in the South," eds. Barbara Esrig, Kate Ellison, Merril Mushroom, Rose Norman, special issue, *Sinister Wisdom* 109 (2018): 10.

10. Desmoines, "Notes for a Magazine II," 28.

11. "About the Press: History," Redbone Press, https://www.redbonepress.com/pages/frontpage, accessed May 6, 2019.

12. Charlene Cothran, "Redeemed! 10 Ways to Get Out of the Gay Life, If You Want Out," *Venus,* February 9, 2007, 99. For further reactions, see responses from one LGBT online community at Karman Kregloe, "Don't Quote Me: Selling Out to God," *AfterEllen,* April 17, 2007, https://www.afterellen.com/people/10089-dont-quote-me-selling-out-to-god#GKYmgYsbpgJYXsA.

13. Harker, *The Lesbian South,* 7.

14. Alexis De Veaux, *Warrior Poet: A Biography of Audre Lorde* (New York: W. W. Norton, 2006), 95.

15. Claudia Tate, ed., *Black Women Writers at Work* (New York: Continuum 1983), 100–16. See also Audre Lorde, "My Words Will Be

There," in *Black Women Writers, 1950–1980: A Critical Evaluation*, ed. Mari Evans (New York: Anchor Books, 1984), 261–68.

16. S. Amdt. 420 to H.R. 2788, https://www.congress.gov/amendment/101st-congress/senate-amendment/420/text.

17. Erik Ose, "Jesse Helms' Shameful Legacy Can't Be White-washed," *Huffpost*, July 21, 2008, updated December 6, 2017, https://www.huffingtonpost.com/erik-ose/jesse-helms-shameful-lega_b_111791.html; also see *Dear Jesse*, directed by Tim Kirkman, 1998.

18. Audre Lorde, "Jessehelms," *Callaloo* 14, no. 1 (Winter 1991): 60–61.

19. Ann Shockley, *Celebrating Hotchclaw* (Rehoboth Beach, DE: A&M Books, 2005), 90.

20. Shockley, *Celebrating Hotchclaw*, 102–3.

21. "LGBTA Center Opens," *NCCU News*, June 17, 2013. www.nccu.edu/news/index.cfm?ID = 41797D03-D007-D7DA-A96557F0CD41A031, accessed May 6, 2019.

22. "LGBTA Center Opens," *NCCU News*, June 17, 2013, www.nccu.edu/news/index.cfm?ID=41797D03-D007-D7DA-A96557F0CD41A031.

23. Perla M. Guerrero, *Nuevo South: Latinas/os, Asians, and the Remaking of Place* (Austin, University of Texas Press, 2017), 9.

24. "About Us," Cocks Not Glocks, http://cocksnotglocks.org/about, accessed May 6, 2019,

25. Luna Malbroux, "Mapping Privilege: What's the Difference between a Gun and a Sex Toy?" *KQED Arts*, May 10, 2017, https://www.kqed.org/pop/78775/mapping-privilege-whats-the-difference-between-a-gun-and-a-sex-toy.

26. Gail Sheehy, "Gun Control Movement Gains A Few Hard Inches," *Jezebel*, August 29, 2016, https://jezebel.com/the-gun-control-movement-gains-a-few-hard-inches-at-ut-1785889695.

27. Sheehy, "Gun Control Movement."

28. Guerrero, *Nuevo South*, 14.

29. Karen Guan, "Bringing Dildos to a Gun Fight," *Study Break*, December 1, 2017, https://studybreaks.com/students/ana-lopez-cocks-not-glocks/.

30. Hannah Smothers, "How a Group of College Girls in Texas Became a National Harassment Target for Guns-Rights Activists," *Cosmopolitan*, September 23, 2016, https://www.cosmopolitan.com/sex-love /a3273931/cocks-not-glocks-protest-texas-harassment/, emphasis mine.

31. See Jessica Valenti, "'Rejection Killings' Need to Be Tracked," *Medium*, November 21, 2018, https://medium.com/s/jessica-valenti /revenge-killings-need-to-be-tracked-37e78a1cf6ce.

32. Alex Samuels, "UT-Austin Students Snatch Up Free Dildos for Gun Protest," *Texas Tribune*, August 23, 2016, https://www .texastribune.org/2016/08/23/students-distribute-4500-sex-toys/.

33. In addition to "Between Women," a web series set in Atlanta, "Two and Fro," "Jessamyn Explains It All," and "Neck of the Woods" are amazing southern queer podcasts.

34. See two informative documentaries on the Johns Committee: *The Committee,* directed by Robert Cassanello and Lisa Mills, 2012, and *Behind Closed Doors: The Dark Legacy of the Johns Committee,* directed by Allyson A. Beutke, 2000.

35. Paulo Freire, *Pedagogy of Indignation* (New York: Routledge, 2016), 15.

CHAPTER THREE

1. Jodi A. Byrd, *Transit of Empire: Indigenous Critiques of Colonialism* (Minneapolis: University of Minnesota Press, 2011), xix.

2. Byrd, *Transit of Empire*, xxx.

3. Cathy J. Cohen, "Punks, Bulldaggers, and Welfare Queens: The Radical Potential of Queer Politics?" *GLQ: A Journal of Lesbian and Gay Studies* 3, no. 4 (January 1997): 437–65, 455.

4. "Commemorative Landscapes," Documenting the American South, https://docsouth.unc.edu/commland/monument/301/, accessed May 7, 2019.

5. Scott Lauria Morgensen, *Spaces between Us: Queer Settler Colonialism and Indigenous Decolonization* (Minneapolis: University of Minnesota Press, 2011), 34.

6. "Company Information," Adam & Eve (website), https://www .adameve.com/t-company_info.aspx, accessed May 7, 2019.

7. Philip D. Harvey, *The Government vs. Erotica: The Siege of Adam & Eve* (New York: Prometheus Books, 2001), 41.

8. Harvey, *Government vs. Erotica*, 45.

9. Tiya Miles, "Uncle Tom Was an Indian: Tracing the Red in Black Slavery," in *Confounding the Color Line: Indian-Black Relations in Multidisciplinary Perspective*, ed. James Brooks, 137–60 (Lincoln: University of Nebraska Press, 2002)," 145.

10. Kirsten Fischer, *Suspect Relations: Sex, Race, and Resistance in Colonial North Carolina* (Ithaca, NY: Cornell University Press, 2001), 123.

11. Lesley M. Graybeal, "'Too Light to Be Black, Too Dark to Be White': Redefining Occaneechi Identity through Community Education," *Native South* 5 (2012): 95–122, 102.

12. Mark Rifkin, "Settler Common sense," *Settler Colonial Studies* 3, no. 3–4 (2013): 322–40.

13. Graybeal, "Too Light," 106.

14. "The Trials of Adam and Eve," *Newsweek*, January 6, 1991, https://www.newsweek.com/trials-adam-eve-202686.

15. Harvey, *Government vs. Erotica*, 26.

16. Harvey, *Government vs. Erotica*, 31.

17. Harvey, *Government vs. Erotica*, 59–56.

18. Laurel Ferejohn, "Our Own Place," *Sinister Wisdom* 109 (2018): 79.

19. Ferejohn, "Our Own Place," 80.

20. "Mandy Carter Interview (March 26, 2013)," in "Southern Lesbian-Feminist Herstory Online Supplement," *Sinister Wisdom* 93, www.sinisterwisdom.org/SW93Supplement/Carter.

21. "About," Southerners on New Ground (website), http://southernersonnewground.org/about/, accessed May 7, 2019.

22. "Pat Hussain Interview (May 6, 2013)," in "Southern Lesbian-Feminist Herstory Online Supplement," *Sinister Wisdom* 93, www.sinisterwisdom.org/SW93Supplement/Hussain.

23. "Mandy Carter Interview."

24. In my own interview with Carter, I asked her if there was a failure that she felt like the organization had learned from. Specifically, she referred to calling people to mobilize for the Mt. Olive Pickle boycott. Carter explained that the Mt. Olive Pickle labor dispute and unionization efforts was one such issue in which the group attempted

and failed to successfully organize. She admits underestimating how much work they needed to do to educate themselves and others about the intersection of race and class.

25. "About," Southerners on New Ground.

26. "Pat Hussain Interview."

27. "Joan Garner Interview (April 12 2013)," in "Southern Lesbian-Feminist Herstory Online Supplement," *Sinister Wisdom* 93, www.sinisterwisdom.org/SW93Supplement/Garner.

28. Liz Bondi, "Gender Divisions and Gentrification: A Critique." *Transactions of the Institute of British Geographers* 16, no. 2 (1991): 194.

29. Jade River, "Mother's Brew and Louisville's Lesbian Feminist Union," *Sinister Wisdom* 109 (2018): 31.

30. River, "Mother's Brew," 32.

31. "Pat Hussain Interview."

32. Jaye Vaughn, "Cedar Chest," *Sinister Wisdom* 109 (2018): 93.

33. River, "Mother's Brew," 33.

34. Gayle S. Rubin, *Deviations: A Gayle Rubin Reader* (Durham, NC: Duke University Press, 2011), 341–45, 356.

35. "Sims, Mary," in "Southern Lesbian-Feminist Herstory Online Supplement," *Sinister Wisdom* 93, www.sinisterwisdom.org/SW93 Supplement/Sims.

36. Bonnie Jean Gabel, "Conjuring: New Orleans Dyke Bar Project," *Sinister Wisdom* 109 (2018): 152–53.

37. The project was created by Los Angeles-based developer Boom Communities, Inc., architect Matthew Hoffman of Hollwich Kushner, and ten architecture firms, half from New York, half from Europe and California. Anna Almendrala, "BOOM! A Bold New Community In Palm Springs," *HuffPost*, February 15, 2011, updated May 25, 2011, https://www.huffingtonpost.com/2011/02/15/boom-retirement-community_n_823535.html.

38. "We Broke Ground!" Village Hearth Cohousing, https://www.villagehearthcohousing.com/we-break-ground.html, accessed May 7, 2019.

39. For slideshows of designs, see "BOOM Community," *ArchDaily*, February 12, 2011, https://www.archdaily.com/111253/boom-community,

accessed May 7, 2019; and "BOOM! A Bold New Community In Palm Springs," *HuffPost*, February 15, 2011, https://www.huffingtonpost.com /2011/02/15/boom-retirement-community_n_823535.html?slideshow=true #gallery/5be2d4d0e4b028402f7ef8bd/0, accessed May 7, 2019.

40. Ken Herman, "Gov. Abbott Says Houston Has More Brothels than Starbucks," *Statesman,* July 5, 2018, https://www.statesman.com /news/20180705/herman-gov-abbott-says-houston-has-more-brothels-than-starbucks.

41. Kamala Kempadoo, *Sexing the Caribbean: Gender, Race, and Sexual Labor* (New York: Routledge, 2004), 2.

42. Carole S. Vance, "Innocence and Experience: Melodramatic Narratives of Sex Trafficking and Their Consequences for Law and Policy," *History of the Present* 2, no. 2 (2012): 200–18, 202.

43. Vance, "Innocence and Experience," 201.

44. M. Jacqui Alexander, *Pedagogies of Crossing: Meditations on Feminism, Sexual Politics, Memory, and the Sacred* (Durham, NC: Duke University Press, 2005), 294.

45. W. Garner Selby, "Greg Abbott Says Houston Is Home to More Brothels than Starbucks Stores," *PolitiFact,* July 13, 2018, https://www .politifact.com/texas/statements/2018/jul/13/greg-abbott/greg-abbott-houston-home-more-brothels-starbucks-t/.

46. Emily Shugerman, "Houston Lawmakers Aim to Block First U.S. Sex Robot Brothel," *The Daily Beast,* October 1, 2018, https://www .thedailybeast.com/houston-lawmakers-aim-to-block-first-us-sex-robot-brothel; and Dan Solomon, "Everything You Should Know About The Proposed Sex Robot Brothel in Houston," *Texas Monthly,* October 3, 2018, https://www.texasmonthly.com/the-culture/everything-need-know-sex-robot-brothel-opening-houston/.

47. Mayra Moreno, "Houston Council Set to Vote on Sex Robot Brothel Ban," *ABC13,* October 1, 2018, https://abc13.com/technology /sex-robot-shop-owner-disputes-human-trafficking-claim/4384888/.

48. FOSTA, the Fight Online Sex Trafficking Act, was the House bill and SESTA, the Stop Enabling Sex Traffickers Act, was the Senate bill; both became law in 2018. Kimberly Lawson, "'We Are Not Victims': How Sex Workers Are Mobilizing Across the Country," *Vice,*

May 30, 2018, https://broadly.vice.com/en_us/article/kzk37e/we-are-not-victims-how-sex-workers-are-mobilizing-across-the-country\.

49. Laura LeMoon, "SESTA Won't Stop Sex Trafficking, but It Will Kill Sex Workers," *Vice*, April 26, 2018, https://broadly.vice.com/en_us/article/pax5pv/sesta-wont-stop-sex-trafficking-but-it-will-kill-sex-workers.

50. "What Is Solicitation of Crime Against Nature (SCAN)?" Women with a Vision (website), wwav-no.org/no-justice/scan, accessed May 7, 2019.

51. Alex Woodward, "Women with a Vision Cope with Arson," *The Advocate*, July 16, 2012, https://www.theadvocate.com/gambit/new_orleans/news/article_613b9055-eaee-5a10-910b-64ef2fc7f15b.html.

CHAPTER FOUR

1. Jenny Jarvie, "Stacey Abrams Weighs in on Abortion Bans, Boycotts and California," *Los Angeles Times*, May 15, 2019, https://www.latimes.com/politics/la-na-stacey-abrams-abortion-film-boycott-georgia-california-20180515-story.html.

2. "Reproductive Health. Rights. Justice," Afiya Center (website), https://theafiyacenter.org/about/, accessed May 7, 2019.

3. Centers for Disease Control and Prevention, "Pregnancy Mortality Surveillance System," https://www.cdc.gov/reproductivehealth/maternalinfanthealth/pregnancy-mortality-surveillance-system.htm, accessed June 5, 2019.

4. For the text of overturned Texas bill HB2, see H.B. No. 2, https://capitol.texas.gov/tlodocs/832/billtext/html/HB00002F.HTM.

5. Audrey Carlsen, "What It Takes to Get an Abortion," *New York Times,* July 20, 2018, https://www.nytimes.com/interactive/2018/07/20/us/mississippi-abortion-restrictions.html.

6. K. K. Rebecca Lai, "Abortion Bans: Nine States Have Passed Bills to Limit the Procedure This Year," *New York Times,* May 29, 2019, https://www.nytimes.com/interactive/2019/us/abortion-laws-states.html.

7. See Amy Harmon, "'Fetal Heartbeat' vs. 'Forced Pregnancy': The Language Wars of Abortion Debate," *New York Times*, May 22,

2019, www.nytimes.com/2019/05/22/us/fetal-heartbeat-forced-pregnancy.html.

8. See Georgia General Assembly, "2019–2020 Regular Session: HB 481 Living Infants Fairness and Equality (LIFE) Act," www.legis.ga.gov/Legislation/en-US/display/20192020/HB/481.

9. Terry Ellis Nicquel, "'Today is a Dark Day for Women': Planned Parenthood Vows to Challenge Alabama Abortion Ban," *USA Today*, May 15. 2019, https://www.usatoday.com/story/news/nation/2019/05/15/alabama-abortion-law-planned-parenthood-laments-dark-day-women/3678059002/.

10. Cathy J. Cohen, "Punks, Bulldaggers, and Welfare Queens: The Radical Potential of Queer Politics?" *GLQ: A Journal of Lesbian and Gay Studies* 3, no. 4 (January 1997): 437–65, 453

11. Willie Parker, *Life's Work: A Moral Argument for Choice* (New York: 37 Ink, 2017), 221–22.

12. Parker, *Life's Work*, 64.

13. Parker, *Life's Work*, 155.

14. See "Southern Project," Religious Coalition for Reproductive Choice (website), http://rcrc.org/southern-project/, accessed June 5, 2019.

15. Parker, *Life's Work,* 158.

16. Parker, *Life's Work*, 164.

17. Parker, *Life's Work*, 167.

18. Parker, *Life's Work*, 126.

19. Ashon T. Crawley, "Circum-Religious Performance: Queer(ed) Black Bodies and the Black Church," *Theology and Sexuality* 14, no. 2 (January 1, 2008): 201–22, 202.

20. James H. Ferguson, "Mississippi Midwives," *Journal of the History of Medicine and Allied Sciences* 5 (Winter 1950): 85–95, 86.

21. Ferguson, "Mississippi Midwives," 85.

22. Byllye Y. Avery, interview by Loretta Ross, July 21–22, 2005, transcript, Voices of Feminism Oral History Project, Sophia Smith Collection, Smith College, Northampton, MA, https://www.smith.edu/libraries/libs/ssc/vof/transcripts/Avery.pdf.

23. Avery, interview, 15.

24. Avery, interview, 16.

25. Avery, interview, 16–17, 21–22.

26. Avery, interview, 17.

27. "Byllye Avery Interview (February 2013)," in "Southern Lesbian-Feminist Herstory Online Supplement," *Sinister Wisdom* 93, www.sinisterwisdom.org/SW93Supplement/Avery.

28. See SisterSong's mission statement and summary of programs, at https://www.sistersong.net/, accessed May 7, 2019.

29. SisterSong provides a detailed analysis and summary of how it helped to defeat the bill at "Our History," #TrustBlackWomen (website), https://trustblackwomen.org/our-roots/, accessed May 7, 2019.

30. See the Human Rights Campaign summary: Hayley Miller, "Mississippi's H.B. 1523 Cleared to Become the Worst Anti-LGBTQ State Law in the U.S.," Human Rights Campaign (blog), June 22, 2017, https://www.hrc.org/blog/mississippis-h.b.-1523-cleared-to-become-the-worst-anti-lgbtq-state-law-in.

31. Nick Morrow, "House Appropriations GOP Adopt License to Discriminate Amendment," Human Rights Campaign (blog), July 11, 2018, https://www.hrc.org/blog/house-appropriations-republicans-adopt-a-license-to-discriminate-amendment.

32. "Take Action," The New Black (website), www.newblackfilm.com/take-action/, accessed May 7, 2019.

33. "Our Programs," Afiya Center (website), https://www.theafiyacenter.org/actions, accessed May 7, 2019.

34. Kimberley Richards, "Reproductive Justice Activist Explains Why Black Leaders Are Key to Abortion Rights," *Huff Post Online,* May 22, 2019, https://www.huffpost.com/entry/abortion-rights-black-leadership-protests_n_5ce45684e4b06f64624c1fb3?fbclid=IwAR18v4Kz6ivD5pTRzi_MvQ8ZGxO2gXjQAJCh5DPi-lQFXcpwxNyefUTGWE0.

35. See Lizzie Presser, "Whatever's Your Darkest Question, You Can Ask Me," *The California Sunday Magazine,* March 28, 2018, https://story.californiasunday.com/abortion-providers, for a compelling exposé on underground networks of abortion training that exceeds digital discussions of the #AuntieNetwork and historical accounts of the Jane Collective in Chicago.

36. Anita Bryant and Bob Green, *At Any Cost* (New York: Fleming H. Revell, 1978), 111.

37. Assata Shakur, *Assata: An Autobiography* (Chicago: Lawrence Hill Books, 2001), 152.

38. Shakur, *Assata*, 155.

39. According to Stefano Harney and Fred Moten, *Undercommons: Fugitive Planning and Black Study* (Wivenhoe, England/Port Watson, NY: Minor Compositions, 2013), study and planning create autonomous and critically ethical modes of being that counter the coercive powers of policy steeped in institutional authority.

CHAPTER FIVE

1. Jedediah Purdy, "Transgender Rights and the End of the New South," *New Yorker*, May 20, 2016, https://www.newyorker.com/news/news-desk/how-north-carolina-governor-pat-mccrory-stumbled-on-transgender-rights.

2. Joellen Kralik, "'Bathroom Bill' Legislative Tracking," National Conference of State Legislatures, July 28, 2017, www.ncsl.org/research/education/-bathroom-bill-legislative-tracking635951130.aspx, accessed May 7, 2019.

3. General Assembly of North Carolina, "Session Law 2016-3-House Bill 2."

4. Cathy J. Cohen, "Punks, Bulldaggers, and Welfare Queens: The Radical Potential of Queer Politics?" *GLQ: A Journal of Lesbian and Gay Studies* 3, no. 4 (January 1997): 437–65, 462.

5. Romans 6:23.

6. Tim Fitzsimons, "String of Transgender Murders Could Be the Work of a Serial Killer, Activists Fear," *NBC*, June 26, 2018, https://www.nbcnews.com/feature/nbc-out/string-transgender-murders-could-be-work-serial-killer-activists-fear-n886801.

7. Ashon T. Crawley, *BlackPentecostal Breath: The Aesthetics of Possibility* (New York: Fordham University Press, 2017), 42.

8. Dan Scanlan and Emily Sullivan, "Transgender Concerns Heard at Sheriff's Forum," *Florida Times Union*, August 3, 2018.

9. *The Gospel According to Andre,* directed by Kate Novack, 2017.

10. Noah Lehava, "Five Minutes with André Leon Talley," *Coveteur*, October 26, 2017, http://coveteur.com/2017/10/26/andre-leon-talley-documentary/.

11. "Little Axe," *We've Been Around* (short film series), episode 4 (Beverly Hills, CA: 11B Productions, 2016); and Oliver Gettell, "*Little Axe* Illuminates Transgender Gospel Singer Willmer Broadnax," *Entertainment Weekly*, March 1, 2016, https://ew.com/article/2016/03/01/little-axe-transgender-gospel-singer-short-film/.

12. Ashon T. Crawley, "Breathing Flesh and the Sound of Black Pentecostalism," *Theology and Sexuality* 19, no. 1 (January 2013): 49–60, 58.

13. See Marlon Rachquel Moore, *In the Life and in the Spirit: Homoerotic Spirituality in African American Literature* (Albany, NY: SUNY Press, 2015).

14. Big Freedia was the other. Mykki Blanco split time between California, Raleigh, NC, and New York.

15. See Eric Shorey, "Gay Rapper Big Momma: 'I Was Never the Type to Be Put in a Box,'" *NewNowNext*, December 29, 2014, www.newnownext.com/gay-rapper-big-momma-i-was-never-the-type-to-be-put-in-a-box/12/2014/.

16. "Big Momma," Last.fm (website), version 2, edited by "NabilBashir," https://www.last.fm/music/Big+Momma/+wiki, accessed May 7, 2019.

17. David Scott, "The Re-enchantment of Humanism: An Interview with Sylvia Wynter," *Small Axe* 8 (September 2000): 175.

18. "Big Momma," *Mommie Dearest,* 2013.

19. "Big Freedia Queen Diva," interview with Kimball Allen, August 20, 2013, video, 8:00, https://www.youtube.com/watch?v=lTu2dV3kfIo, accessed May 7, 2019.

20. "Big Freedia Sentenced for Section 8 Fraud," *States News Service*, August 25, 2016. Matt Sledge, "Feds Charge Big Freedia with Felony Theft, Reportedly Say She Lied about Income for Section 8 Housing," *The New Orleans Advocate,* March 3, 2016, https://www.theadvocate.com/new_orleans/news/article_0668c6b6-ec55-5921-9257-7de98b04f578.html.

21. "Big Freedia Takes 'Full Responsibility,'" *Louisiana Weekly*, March 7, 2016, http://www.louisianaweekly.com/big-freedia-takes-full-responsibility/.

22. See Cahshauna Hill's statement in Brentin Mock, "Why Big Freedia Shouldn't Do Jail Time Over Housing Vouchers," *CityLab*, March 17, 2016, https://www.citylab.com/equity/2016/03/why-big-freedia-shouldnt-do-jail-time-over-housing-vouchers-fraud/474159/.

23. Daniel Kreps, "Big Freedia Reschedules Mississippi Show Canceled Due to Twerking," *Rolling Stone*, March 4, 2016, https://www.rollingstone.com/music/music-news/big-freedia-reschedules-mississippi-show-canceled-due-to-twerking-236848/.

24. Ashon T. Crawley, "Circum-Religious Performance: Queer(ed) Black Bodies and the Black Church," *Theology and Sexuality* 14, no. 2 (January 1, 2008): 201–22, 202.

CODA

1. Gloria Anzaldúa, *Borderlands/La Frontera: The New Mestiza*, 2nd ed. (San Francisco: Aunt Lute Books, 1999), 37–38.

2. Gloria Anzaldúa, "La Prieta," in *This Bridge Called My Back: Writings by Radical Women of Color*, eds. Cherríe Moraga and Gloria Anzaldúa (New York: Kitchen Table, Women of Color Press, 1983), 205.

3. "Testimony of Rochelle M. Garza, Managing Attorney, Garza & Garza Law, PLLC, before the Committee on the Judiciary, United States Senate, Hearing on the Nomination of Brett Kavanaugh to the Supreme Court of the United States," September 7, 2018, https://www.judiciary.senate.gov/imo/media/doc/Garza%20Testimony.pdf; for video of her testimony, see "Rochelle Garza Testimony," *CSPAN*, September 7, 2018, https://www.c-span.org/video/?c4748267/rochelle-garza-testimony.

4. See Valeria Vera, "Border Patrol's Not-So-Secret: The Normalized Abuse of Migrant Women on the U.S.-Mexico Border," *International Affairs Review* (Fall 2013); and Alice Spire, "Detained then Violated," *The Intercept*, April 11, 2018, https://theintercept.com/2018/04/11/immigration-detention-sexual-abuse-ice-dhs/.

5. HCS SC 529, Georgia Security and Immigration Compliance Act, https://votesmart.org/bill/1127/georgia-security-and-immigration-compliance-act#3229.

6. HB87, Illegal Immigration Reform and Enforcement Act of 2011, http://www.legis.ga.gov/legislation/en-US/display/32190.

7. Irene Browne and Mary Odem, "'Juan Crow' in the Nuevo South? Racialization of Guatemalan and Dominican Immigrants in the Atlanta Metro Area," *Du Bois Review* 9, no. 2 (October 2012): 321–37, 322.

8. Curtis Marez, *Farm Worker Futurism: Speculative Technologies of Resistance* (Minneapolis: University of Minnesota Press, 2016), 119–54.

9. Soon Kyu Choi, Bianca D.M. Wilson, Jama Shelton, and Gary Gates, "Serving Our Youth 2015: The Needs and Experiences of Lesbian, Gay, Bisexual, Transgender, and Questioning Youth Experiencing Homelessness," True Colors Fund, June 2015, 5, https://truecolorsfund.org/wp-content/uploads/2015/05/Serving-Our-Youth-June-2015.pdf.

10. True Colors Fund, "State Index on Youth Homelessness, 2018," 79–80, https://drive.google.com/file/d/14hCgF6gwxF7At2kanWLulciE1NPN-Z5C/view.

11. BreakOUT! and Congress of Day Laborers, *From Vice to ICE: Toolkit,* 2017, p. 4, http://nowcrj.org/wp-content/uploads/2017/06/engVicetoICE_FINAL.pdf.

12. BreakOUT! and Congress of Day Laborers, *From Vice to ICE*, 12.

13. Gayl Jones, *Mosquito* (Boston: Beacon Press, 1999), 616.

14. Jones, *Mosquito*, 307.

GLOSSARY

INTERSECTIONALITY Denotes how oppressions of race, gender, sexuality, ability, nation, and class—and subsequent institutional discourses about them—are linked. Concept is attributed to legal scholar Kimberlee Crenshaw, but existence and praxis of intersectional politics precedes her coinage.

DAWES ACT OF 1887 Used to displace Native Americans and introduce land politics foundational to capitalism and settler colonialism. Allowed the president to begin dividing and allotting land to individual Native people, as opposed to tribes.

DECOLONIZATION Process of undoing or dismantling the structures and systems of oppression enacted through violence, land and labor exploitation, and assimilation into colonizers' languages, cultures, or spiritual practices.

SETTLER COLONIALISM Systemic and structural repression of Indigenous people's culture, normalization of exploitation of land and natural resources.

SETTLER SEXUALITY Biopolitics of settler colonialism in the form of blood ratios that determine access to stolen land politics and regulate Native Americans' sexuality while erasing and invalidating Indigenous people's sexuality and genders.

SPATIALIZATION Denotes how social activities and networking practices operate across or influence the arrangement of space.

KEY FIGURES

GLORIA ANZALDÚA Chicana lesbian feminist, poet, and critical writer
of some of the most significant theories on material and immate-
rial borderlands, multiraciality, marginalization, and sexuality.

BREAKOUT! New Orleans-based community organization whose
vision centers on intervening on the criminalization of
LGBTQ youth.

CATHY COHEN Political scientist, queer theorist, feminist activist,
and University of Chicago professor whose work challenges
deracinated models of queerness and classless approaches to
heteronormativity, silence and stigma around HIV/AIDS, and
dismissal of youth-based resistance.

MILLIE JACKSON R&B and soul singer of the 1970s whose racy lyrics
and bawdy performances distinguished her from other singers of
her time and made her significant to women rappers' performances of sexual bravado in hip-hop.

JESSICA JIN Creator of Cocks Not Glocks campaign, which sought to
protest campus carry laws in Texas using sex toys.

AUDRE LORDE Caribbean American writer, activist, and teacher
whose lesbian feminist ideals challenged heteropatriarchy and
white supremacy.

ANN ALLEN SHOCKLEY Southern writer, librarian, and archivist. One
of the earliest Black women writers to publish novels centered on
lesbian life and experience.

SISTERSONG Women of color reproductive justice organization in
Atlanta serving a national membership. Focus is on curtailing
institutional policies disproportionately impacting women of color
and Indigenous women's reproductive freedom since 1997.

SOUTHERNERS ON NEW GROUND Antiracist, queer-feminist social
justice organization founded in 1993 with a mission to transform
outdated southern politics into radical coalitional politics
informed by intersectionality and LGBTQ perspectives.

WOMEN WITH A VISION Grassroots New Orleans community-based
nonprofit organization founded in 1989 to address women's health,
LGBTQ population needs, and decriminalization of sex work.

SELECTED BIBLIOGRAPHY

Alexander, M. Jacqui. *Pedagogies of Crossing: Meditations on Feminism, Sexual Politics, Memory, and the Sacred*. Durham, NC: Duke University Press, 2005.

Anzaldúa, Gloria. *Borderlands/La Frontera: The New Mestiza*. 2nd ed. San Francisco: Aunt Lute Books, 1999.

Anzaldúa, Gloria, and AnaLouise Keating. *The Gloria Anzaldúa Reader*. Durham, NC: Duke University Press, 2009.

Browne, Irene, and Mary Odem. "'Juan Crow' in the Nuevo South? Racialization of Guatemalan and Dominican Immigrants in the Atlanta Metro Area." *Du Bois Review* 9, no. 2 (October 2012): 321–37.

Byrd, Jodi A. *The Transit of Empire: Indigenous Critiques of Colonialism*. Minneapolis: University of Minnesota Press, 2011.

Cohen, Cathy J. *The Boundaries of Blackness: AIDS and the Breakdown of Black Politics*. Chicago: University of Chicago Press, 2009.

———. "Deviance as Resistance: A New Research Agenda for the Study of Black Politics." *Du Bois Review* 1, no. 1 (March 2004): 27–45.

———. "Punks, Bulldaggers, and Welfare Queens: The Radical Potential of Queer Politics?" *GLQ: A Journal of Lesbian and Gay Studies* 3, no. 4 (January 1997): 437–65.

Cohn, Deborah N., and Jon Smith. *Look Away! The U.S. South in New World Studies*. Durham, NC: Duke University Press, 2004.

Crawley, Ashon T. *BlackPentecostal Breath: The Aesthetics of Possibility*. New York: Fordham University Press, 2017.

———. "Breathing Flesh and the Sound of Black Pentecostalism." *Theology and Sexuality* 19, no. 1 (January 2013): 49–60.

———. "Circum-Religious Performance: Queer(ed) Black Bodies and the Black Church." *Theology and Sexuality* 14, no. 2 (January 1, 2008): 201–22.

Davis, Thadious M. *Southscapes: Geographies of Race, Region, and Literature*. Chapel Hill: University of North Carolina Press, 2011.

Forman, James. "Black Manifesto." In *Reparations for Slavery: A Reader*, edited by Ronald P. Salzberger and Mary C. Turck, 70–75. Lanham, MD: Rowman and Littlefield Publishers, 2004.

Harker, Jaime. *The Lesbian South: Southern Feminists, the Women in Print Movement, and the Queer Literary Canon*. Chapel Hill: University of North Carolina Press, 2018.

Jones, Gayl. *Mosquito*. Boston: Beacon Press, 1999.

Kempadoo, Kamala. *Sexing the Caribbean: Gender, Race, and Sexual Labor*. New York: Routledge, 2004.

Lyon, Janet. *Manifestoes: Provocations of the Modern*. Ithaca, NY: Cornell University Press, 1999.

Marez, Curtis. *Farm Worker Futurism: Speculative Technologies of Resistance*. Minneapolis: University of Minnesota Press, 2016.

Moraga, Cherríe, and Gloria Anzaldúa, eds. *This Bridge Called My Back: Writings by Radical Women of Color*. New York: Kitchen Table, Women of Color Press, 1983.

Morgensen, Scott Lauria. *Spaces between Us: Queer Settler Colonialism and Indigenous Decolonization*. Minneapolis: University of Minnesota Press, 2011.

Shakur, Assata. *Assata: An Autobiography*. Chicago: Lawrence Hill Books, 2001.

Shockley, Ann Allen. *Celebrating Hotchclaw*. Rehoboth Beach, DE: A&M Books, 2005.

Trambley, Estela Portillo. "If It Weren't for the Honeysuckle." In *Rain of Scorpions and Other Stories,* 47–70. Clasicos Chicanos/Chicano Classics. Tempe: Bilingual Press, 1993.

Vargas, Deborah R. "Ruminations on *Lo Sucio* as a Latino Queer Analytic." *American Quarterly* 66, no. 3 (September 2014): 715–26.

Founded in 1893,
UNIVERSITY OF CALIFORNIA PRESS
publishes bold, progressive books and journals
on topics in the arts, humanities, social sciences,
and natural sciences—with a focus on social
justice issues—that inspire thought and action
among readers worldwide.

The UC PRESS FOUNDATION
raises funds to uphold the press's vital role
as an independent, nonprofit publisher, and
receives philanthropic support from a wide
range of individuals and institutions—and from
committed readers like you. To learn more, visit
ucpress.edu/supportus.